de Gruyter Studies in Organization 58

On Studying Organizational Cultures

de Gruyter Studies in Organization

Organizational Theory and Research

This de Gruyter Series aims at publishing theoretical and methodological studies of organizations as well as research findings, which yield insight in and knowledge about organizations. The whole spectrum of perspectives will be considered: organizational analyses rooted in the sociological as well as the economic tradition, from a socio-psychological or a political science angle, mainstream as well as critical or ethnomethodological contributions. Equally, all kinds of organizations will be considered: firms, public agencies, non-profit institutions, voluntary associations, inter-organizational networks, supra-national organizations etc.

Emphasis is on publication of *new* contributions, or significant revisions of existing approaches. However, summaries or critical reflections on current thinking and research will also be considered.

This series represents an effort to advance the social scientific study of organizations across national boundaries and academic disciplines. An Advisory Board consisting of representatives of a variety of perspectives and from different cultural areas is responsible for achieving this task.

This series addresses organization researchers within and outside universities, but also practitioners who have an interest in grounding their work on recent social scientific knowledge and insights.

Majken Schultz

On Studying Organizational Cultures

Diagnosis and Understanding

Walter de Gruyter · Berlin · New York 1995

Majken Schultz, Associate Professor, PhD, Copenhagen Business School, Institute of Organization and Industrial Sociology Copenhagen, Denmark

With 15 tables, 19 figures, and 3 diagrams

⊗ Printed on acid-free paper which falls within the guidelines of the ANSI to ensure permanence and durability.

Library of Congress Cataloging-in-Publication Data

Schultz, Majken.
On studying organizational cultures : diagnosis and understanding / Majken Schultz.
p. cm. – (De Gruyter studies in organization ; 58)
Includes bibliographical references.
ISBN 3-11-014137-X (alk. paper)
ISBN 3-11-014649-5 (pbk.)
1. Corporate culture. 2. Business anthropology. I. Title. II. Series.
HD58.7.S347 1994
302.3′5–dc20 94-18283
CIP

Die Deutsche Bibliothek – Cataloging-in-Publication Data

Schultz, Majken:
On studying organizational cultures : diagnosis and understanding / Majken Schultz. – Berlin ; New York : de Gruyter, 1994
(De Gruyter studies in organization ; 58)
ISBN 3-11-014137-X (geb.)
ISBN 3-11-014649-5 (brosch.)
NE: GT

Typesetting: Converted by Knipp Satz und Bild digital, Dortmund – Printing: Gerike GmbH, Berlin. – Binding: D. Mikolai, Berlin. – Cover Design: Johannes Rother, Berlin.
Printed in Germany.

Contents

Introduction

There is a wealth of literature on organizational culture with many competing theoretical views of the culture concept and its importance. However, there are far fewer examples of how actual organizational cultures can be studied and described in real life. It is a separate, quite different task to specify more precisely the theoretical concepts of culture and how these concepts might be applied to the analysis of organizations. Only then is it possible to evaluate different views of culture and to discover how organizational culture may improve our understanding of organizations.

This book focuses on the empirical analysis of organizational culture by applying two distinct views of culture to the analysis of the same organization. The book fills a gap in the organizational culture literature by combining theoretical modelling with empirical application. Two significant theoretical perspectives are systematically applied in order to enable the reader to carry out comparable cultural analyses. The book is very useful as a textbook at the graduate level. It offers a clear structuring of cultural issues, which can serve as the outline of an organizational culture course. In addition, the book addresses consultants and managers in need of a tool-kit for analyzing organizational culture. The book is more comprehensive than the 'quick fix' literature and it provides guidelines and examples to follow in the concrete analysis and change of organizational culture.

Chapter 1 provides a quick overview of the field and the most important theoretical paradigms within culture theory. First, the chapter discusses how the concept of culture has been located within organization theory and, secondly, different theoretical approaches to the study of organizational culture are introduced. Based on this overview, the chapter argues why the functionalist and the symbolic perspectives have been chosen for the following theoretical examination and empirical analysis.

Chapter 2 deals specifically with the functionalist perspective of culture and its theoretical assumptions. The analysis of functionalism draws upon the work of E. Schein (1984; 1985a; 1992), but adds a number of new theoretical arguments and provides an analytical model (the funnel) for the empirical analysis. This model combines the levels and functions of culture, which have so far not been integrated in the empirical studies of culture.

The empirical application of the funnel model is carried out in Chapter 3. The chapter offers a very systematic analysis of the organizational culture and, opposed to most Scheinian work, a full scale cultural analysis is conducted. Thus, apart from the cultural paradigm, the relations between the various levels of culture are specified. Due to the general and systematic character of a functionalist analysis, only one empirical example is provided. The organization analyzed is a department within a Danish government ministry, the department being the highest level administrative unit placed directly under the politically appointed minister.

Chapter 4 discusses the symbolic cultural perspective. The chapter contains an overview of the key concepts and interpretative frameworks, which have been dominating within symbolic theory. Opposed to the functionalist perspective which builds on one primary source, the symbolic perspective draws on numerous contributions within anthropology, semiotics and organizational theory. However, the main focus is still the empirical application of the theoretical contributions. The chapter suggests a new empirical framework for conducting cultural interpretations (the spiral), which highlights the associative qualities of a symbolic way of reading culture.

Here, in Chapter 5, the symbolic perspective is illustrated in two different empirical settings. The first setting is the department, which is also analyzed in Chapter 2, whereas the second organization is a subordinate directorate. The reason for providing two examples of cultural interpretation is that the symbolic perspective, different from the functionalist one, is conducted according to the uniqueness of the organization studied. Each empirical setting has its own key symbols, which are reflected in the way the symbolic perspective is applied empirically. As the symbolic perspective offers a new and innovative methodology, the spiral is discussed separately at the end of the chapter.

The final chapter provides an overview of important theoretical and methodological differences between the two perspectives. Often, the differences between the perspectives have been taken for granted at a general level and have rarely been specified. The specification suggested in this chapter makes it possible to highlight the strengths and weaknesses of each perspective and thus invites the students to further considerations. Finally, some important similarities between the two perspectives are stated on the basis of the recent debate on postmodernism and cultural ambiguity. Thus, although the book focuses on some of the classical perspectives within cultural studies, the final chapter discusses contemporary scholars' critique and self-reflection.

I am especially grateful for the help and support provided by Finn Borum and Jan Molin, Tore Jacob Hegland, Lauge Stetting and P.O. Berg during the process of writing the Danish version of the book. Editing the

English version of the book I have strongly drawn on teaching experiences with Kristian Kreiner and Mary Jo Hatch. A number of the ideas for the revision originate from our joint culture-classes. I am especially grateful to Mary Jo Hatch for her tremendous help and support in rewriting the manuscript. For comments on early drafts I wish to thank Joanne Martin, Debra Meyerson, Edgar Schein and Dvora Yanow. I also want to thank Stephen Sampson, who on top of the translation, has contributed with important remarks. Finally, I want to thank Marianne Risberg who has helped in finishing the manuscript with energy and substantial insight.

Chapter 1
Culture in Organization Theory

Organizational culture focuses on the beliefs, values and meanings used by members of an organization to grasp how the organization's uniqueness originates, evolves, and operates. The concept of organizational culture has received consider able attention within organizational theory in the last decade (Pondy et al., 1983; Frost et al., 1985; Smircich, 1983a; Schein, 1985a; 1992; Alvesson and Berg, 1992; Turner, 1990; Gagliardi, 1992; Martin, 1993; Trice and Beyer, 1993). Researchers, consultants and managers have gravitated to the concept of culture in order to encompass the special way of life and creation of meanings which evolve within an organization.

The concept of culture has emerged as a result of a break with a rationalist, mechanistic conception of organization (Burrell and Morgan, 1979; Morgan, 1986; Scott, 1992). Here, members of organizations have been conceived of as tools for an efficient goal-achievement, calculating organizational behavior from a careful examination of various alternatives within a formal organizational structure. Instead of studying these structural and goal oriented working activities in organizations, the culture concept emphasizes the fundamental frameworks which people take for granted in their social and occupational activities.

The longstanding critique of rationalism within organ izational theory culminates with the concept of culture, but obviously this critique builds on previous organizational theory like early institutionalism (Scott, 1990) and conceptions of organizations as natural systems (Scott, 1992; Morgan, 1986). Within a naturalist framework, the informal and social aspects of organizational life are studied, emphasizing the norms and social roles of the informal structure. However, the concept of organizational culture also differs significantly from notions of the informal organizational structure, which seek to discover actual organizational behavior, whether or not proscribed by formal organizational guidelines. Opposed to the study of both formal and informal organizational behavior, a cultural way of studying organizations is to study the meaning of organizational behavior – or more specifically, the meanings and beliefs which members of organizations assign to organiz ational behavior and how these assigned meanings influence the ways in which they behave themselves.

Here is no single answer as to why the interest in organizational culture internationally arose precisely in the 1980s. Morgan (1986) cites Japan's economic miracle as an important reason why American organization theorists and managers, especially, had focused their attention on the relationship between culture and organization. Japan's explosive economic growth had through the 1970s generated questions concerning Western management techniques and organizational forms and increased interest for acquiring Japanese organizational forms such as quality circles, corporate philosophy, and closer relations between the employees and the organization (Pascale and Athos, 1982; Ouchi, 1981; Vogel, 1979).

Another essential point of departure for the debate on organizational culture was a search for new paths to excellence and efficiency, grasping the complexity of modern organizations and responding to the needs for a challenging and meaningful worklife. The most popular stimulant to these efforts was Peters and Waterman's *In Search of Excellence* (1982), but also Clark (1977), Deal and Kennedy (1982), Hofstede (1980; 1991), Pondy et al. (1983) addressed issues of organizational efficiency and survival. In recent years the efficiency argument has been especially elaborated by Kotter and Heskett (1992) and Denyson (1990). The relationship between the organization and its environments has been improved significantly and simple notions of cultural strengths and weaknesses are related to needs for ongoing change processes in organizations. In the debate on excellent companies, culture is not simply assumed to be a characteristic of the organization but a phenomenon created by the leadership which opens new organizational possibilities: 'Perhaps the most important failing of the narrow view of rationality is not that it is wrong per se, but that it has led to a dramatic imbalance in the way we think about management' (Peters and Waterman, 1982:12).

Thus, after ten years of cultural debate, there is a wealth of literature on organizational culture with many competing theoretical views of the culture concept and its importance (Smircich, 1983a; Putnam, 1983; Frost et al., 1985; 1991; Alvesson and Berg, 1992; Martin, 1993). Numerous attempts have been made to clarify the concept of culture theoretically and to apply it to the analysis of leadership, structure and change of organizations (Kilmann et al., 1985; Schein, 1985a; Hampden-Turner, 1990; French and Bell, 1990).

However, there are far fewer examples of how actual organiz ational cultures can be studied and described in real life. It is a separate, quite different task to specify more precisely the theoretical concepts of culture and how these concepts might be applied to the analysis of organizations. Only then is it possible to evaluate different views of culture and to discover the implications of theoretical distinctions for the concrete insights obtained by cultural analysis. This book elaborates and demonstrates two ways of doing cultural analysis in organizations in order to show the range of opportunities when using the concept of culture in organizational analysis and to allow a comparison of the strengths and weaknesses of each cultural framework.

Due to the culture concept's broad character several unclari fied questions and old controversies within organizational theory are found also in the debate on organizational culture. This chapter attempts briefly to clarify the concept of culture so as to provide the conceptual background for the theoretical and empirical elaboration of cultural analysis. First, the overall position of the culture concept within organizational theory is considered; second, various conceptual typologies of the culture concept itself are summarized highlighting the choices being made in the selection and elaboration of the two cultural perspectives discussed in this book.

Position within Organizational Theory

The Danish author Willy Sørensen in his book *Uden mål – og med* [Without Goal and With (one)], reminds us that culture originally stems from to cultivate: 'The culture concept means cultivating, whether we are cultivating the land or the gods, it is a cultural activity which is being carried out' (Sørensen 1983:7). Morgan refers to the notion: 'the word [culture] has been derived metaphorically from the idea of cultivation, the process of tilling and developing land' (Morgan, 1986:112). The anthropologist Geertz (1973; 1983), who has significantly influenced an interpretative understanding of culture, demonstrates that the culture concept developed in order to distinguish humans from the animal kingdom. In contrast to the regularity of nature, the culture concept has evolved in order to conceptualize man's diversity. The culture concept asserts that we socially construct different understandings of nature and hence, of that reality which surrounds us and which we also help to create.

Thus, in its most general meaning, culture connotes 'that different groups of people have different ways of life' (Morgan, 1986:112), where 'ways of life' are deeply rooted, tradition-bound and stable modes of living transmitted from generation to generation. Different cultural groups have primarily been synonymous with different countries, ethnic groups, tribes, religions, etc. But 'culture' has also attained a wider significance as counter-cultures, subcultures, and the cultures of social classes or groups. In this perspective, interest in cultures within organizations is the latest application of the culture concept and signifies its increasingly broader application.

Hence, apart from previous organizational theory, the concept of culture draws upon theories and insights within anthropology and the humanities (Morgan, 1986; Scott, 1992), and Smircich (1983a) has demonstrated how several controversies in the study of organizational culture are also found within anthropology. Within general organizational theory, culture has among other things been characterized as a new paradigm, a new metaphor or a new approach for understanding organizations. Here, only two significant attempts to locate the concept of culture within general organizational theory will be mentioned.

Culture as a New Metaphor

Morgan divides the understanding of organizations according to the various metaphors which direct and bias the perception of organizational life:

> For the use of metaphors implies a way of thinking and a way of seeing that pervade how we understand our world generally... We use metaphors whenever we attempt to understand one element of experience in terms of another... Many of our taken-for-granted ideas about organizations are metaphorical, even though we may not recognize them as such. For example, we frequently talk about organizations as if they were machines designed to achieve predetermined goals and objectives, and which should operate smoothly and efficiently (Morgan, 1986:13).

The machine and the biological organism are the most recognized metaphors for depicting organizations as rational and natural systems (Scott, 1992). The metaphors direct our focus on the organization's formal and informal structures respectively. Morgan cites culture as a third metaphor which calls attention to the organization's human sides, the latter often being neglected by both the machine and the biological organism metaphors.

The culture metaphor operates neither according to the pre scribed behavior directed toward fulfillment of goals nor according to the informal behavior oriented toward survival (Scott, 1992). Rather, the culture metaphor operates to elaborate the meaning and significance which the members of the organization attach to both the prescribed and the informal behavior. The organization does not exist per se, but is constructed by the organization's members via the meanings and the interpretations which they accord to actions and experience within the organization.

Apart from culture, Morgan discusses several other metaphors for understanding organizations, e.g. organizations as brains, as political systems and as instruments of domination.

Culture as a New Approach

Bolman and Deal (1987), while presenting another conceptualization of organizational theory, define the culture concept as a new and different approach to understanding organizations. They depart from different theoretical frames of reference: 'each frame has its own vision of reality... The theories, or frames, that we use determine what we see and what we do' (Bolman and Deal, 1987:25). The individual frames of reference help structure different approaches to the study of organizations.

The different approaches summarized (Bolman and Deal, 1987:5) include:

1. *Rational approach:* Emphasizes the importance of formal roles and relations. The formal structure is adapted to the organization's technology and environments, dividing responsibility and coordinating activities.
2. *Human resource approach*: Emphasizes relations between human needs and the organization. Each human's needs, feelings, qualifications, and prejudices are at the center of the analysis, stressing the importance of the enrichment of human resources to the organization. Individuals should enjoy their work.
3. *Political approach:* The organization is defined as an arena of conflict over scarce resources, where power and conflicts constantly effect the distribution of scarce resources between individuals and groups. Negotiations, compromises and coalitions characterize the organizations.
4. *Symbolic approach:* Organizations stay together because of shared values and culture rather than objectives and policies. The values are transmitted via rituals, ceremonies, stories, heroes, and myths, as opposed to rules, leadership authority and regulations.

In the description of the symbolic approach, Bolman and Deal emphasize that organizations can be understood as theatres or carnivals, where the individuals play out grand dramas -colorful and meaningful.

Contribution to Organizational Theory

Both usages of the culture concept within organizational theory emphasize its two important contributions.

First, the culture concept has directed our attention to new phenomena in the organization, expanding the field of study. With the help of the culture concept, myths, metaphors, rituals, stories, sagas, clans, heroes, ceremonies, artifacts, world views, ethos and aesthetics have been brought into our understanding of organizations (Trice and Beyer, 1993; Alvesson and Berg, 1992:45-57; Gagliardi, 1992). In the words of John Van Maanen

(1988), organizational culture has made the barroom talk, absurd experiences and good stores of earlier times into legitimate objects of research.

Second, organizational culture has reinterpreted well known phenomena and posed questions about their significance. Formal structure is no longer simply a means of understanding the organization's division of labor and coordination, but also a symbol of the dominant myths about effective organizations (Meyer and Rowan, 1977). The organization's strategic planning is no longer a forum for long term decision making, but also a forum for the interpretation of past events and a signal that the future is important for an organization (Sapienza, 1985). Informal organization is no longer a routinized behavioral pattern, but also a cultural network where priests, spies, storytellers and 'support clubs' translate and transmit the organizationš key values (Deal and Kennedy, 1982).

Cultural Diversity

In spite of the strong interest in organizational culture there has not yet been – and may never be – established a generally accepted conceptual framework for analyzing organizational culture. However, several different theoretical typologies have been elaborated which summarize the various differences in the culture concept. Yet these are seldom in agreement as to which criteria should be applied in the typologizing of an organizational culture (Smircich, 1983a; 1983b; 1985; Allaire and Firsirotu, 1984; Pondy et al., 1983; Alvesson and Berg, 1992; Martin and Meyerson, 1988; Martin, 1993). Here we will discuss three different typologies each emphasizing important differences in the culture debate.

Variable or Metaphor

Smircich (1983a) emphasizes a fundamental difference between the view that organizations *have* culture as opposed to the notion that organizations *are* culture.

Organizations have culture in that culture is seen as one variable among several others; e.g. structure, tasks, actors, and technology in the Leavitt model (Leavitt, 1965). Culture is an attribute of the organization, typically defined as values or attitudes. Smircich differentiates between culture as an independent variable which is accorded the organization via membership and cultural context, and organizational culture as an internal dependent variable formed within the organization. Here, culture is perceived as an instrumental attribute to be acquired and manipulated by members of the organization.

Being a variable implies that culture can be mapped onto a scale. An essential part of cultural analysis therefore consists of outlining the culture in relation to a given scale of values. The two most widely used culture scales are:

1. *Strong and weak cultures* (e. g. Deal and Kennedy, 1982; Kotter and Heskett, 1992), which evaluate the culture's internal consistence and impact on the organization's members;
2. *efficient and inefficient cultures* (e.g. Peters and Waterman, 1982; Denyson, 1990), which evaluate cultures in relation to fulfillment of goals, ability to innovate and strategic capacity.

In the alternative conception organizations are culture. The culture concept works as a root metaphor for understanding the human constructs and expressions in organizations.

> Culture as a root metaphor promotes a view of organizations as expressive forms, manifestations of human consciousness. Organizations are understood and analyzed not mainly in economic or material terms, but in terms of their expressive, ideational and symbolic aspects (Smircich, 1983a:347-348).

As a root metaphor culture cannot be restricted to certain organizational variables, but encompasses the processes by which the organization's members interpret their experiences, how these interpretations are expressed, and how they relate to organizational action.

Both views of organizational culture, however, emphasize organizational culture as something shared by all the organization's members, either in terms of shared values and attitudes, or overlapping interpretative frameworks.

Integration, Differentiation and Ambiguity

Martin and Meyerson (1988), Meyerson (1991), and Martin (1993) have sharply criticized the culture debate's single-minded focus on culture as a cohesive pattern shared by all members of the organization: 'it emphasizes consistency among cultural manifestations and organization-wide consensus among cultural members' (Martin and Meyerson, 1988:102). The culture debate has assumed consistency between cultural manifestations such as values, formal and informal practices, and artifacts like stories, rituals, and jargon, creating an organization-wide consensus between all members of the organization. They characterize the dominant body of theory as an integration paradigm, such that organizational culture is perceived as 'the glue that holds an organization together' (Martin and Meyerson, 1988:103).

Instead, they present two other paradigms for understanding organizational culture: differentiation and ambiguity. These are not exclusive alternatives to the integration paradigm. Rather, they pose other questions in the empirical analysis of organizational culture.

The differentiation paradigm emphasizes the lack of consistency between cultural manifestations and the lack of consensus among the organization's members. The differentiation paradigm typically studies organizational culture in terms of different subcultures.

> The differentiation paradigm stresses inconsistencies, delineates the absence of organization-wide consensus (usually in the form of overlapping, nested subcultures), and stresses nonleader centered sources of cultural content (Martin and Meyerson, 1988:110).

There are, for example, different values and practices concerning equality within the organization studied by Martin and Meyerson, causing the creation of subcultures between different groups of the organization. However, within each subculture consensus between the members of the subculture exist, creating a subcultural consensus. In the culture debate organizational subcultures have been analyzed according to differences in professional backgrounds, functional position in the organization, links to the different business areas, etc. (Gregory, 1983; Van Maanen and Barley, 1985). Also, it has been stressed that subcultures can have various relations to each other, ranging from conflict to peaceful coexistence (Martin and Siehl, 1983; Louis, 1983; Pedersen and Sørensen, 1989).

Both the integration and differentiation paradigms imply clarity among the organization's members about the existence and contents of the cultural manifestations, whether it is shared by all members of the organization or divided between different subcultures. As a third paradigm, Martin and Meyerson therefore introduce ambiguity or fragmentation, which directs our attention to the lack of clarity and the uncertainty, confusion and double meanings which the organizational culture holds for the organization's members:

> A culture viewed from an ambiguity paradigm perspective cannot be characterized as harmonious or conflictful. Instead, individuals share some viewpoints, disagree about some, and are ignorant of or indifferent to others. Consensus, dissensus and confusion coexist, making it difficult to draw cultural and subcultural boundaries (Martin and Meyerson, 1988:117).

The ambiguity paradigm highlights the cultural complexity characterizing many organizations, where constant streams of information, changes in working conditions, and turbulent environments create confusion and uncertainty among the organization's members. If they exist at all, shared understandings become issue-specific and limited to certain organizational situations. In that case an ambiguity paradigm view of a culture would have no universally shared integrating set of values except for one: the very awareness of ambiguity. Here, the ambiguity paradigm reminds of decision theory's garbage can model (March and Olsen, 1976), where decisions result from accidental timing between choice opportunities, solutions, problems, and participants under conditions of high uncertainty.

The ambiguity paradigm raises new questions regarding the limits of the concept of culture; both within anthropology and in the humanities, the culture concept connotes first of all shared characteristics within a group or society. By introducing the ambiguity paradigm Martin and Meyerson point out several important weaknesses in the culture concept's focus on collectivity and integration in organizations, noting that it overlooks the conflicts and confusions which inevitably arise among the organization's members. Thus, confusion, uncertainty, and ambiguity may be essential characteristics of an organizational culture, whereas the completely accidental and contextually bounded creation of meaning may demand a more radical reformulation of the classical manifestations of culture, also found in the analytical model (the matrix framework) developed by Martin and Meyerson (1988).

Rationalism, Functionalism and Symbolism

Finally, the culture debate can be discussed according to various classic perspectives within organizational theory. Although the concept of organizational culture poses new questions to the study of organizations by introducing culture as a new perspective or metaphor replacing organizations as machines (rational perspective) and organism (natural perspective), some of the fundamental assumptions of these two metaphors are also found in the debate on organizational culture. Perspectives are defined by Scott as 'analytical models intended to guide and to interpret empirical research' (1992:55). Here we will discuss three perspectives central to the culture debate, which are summarized in Table 1.1.

Rationalism and functionalism, derived from machine and organic metaphors, respectively, are general perspectives which penetrate much of organizational theory. Thus, although Morgan (1986) and Bolman and Deal (1987) categorize organizational culture as a new metaphor or approach, several preexisting assumptions about organizations are also transferred to the culture concept.

Table 1.1. Theoretical Perspective in the Culture Debate

Perspective	Organizational paradigm	Organizational culture
Rationalism	The organization is a means to efficient achievement.	The culture is a tool tool for achievement of organizational goals.
Functionalism	The organization is a collective which seeks survival by performing necessary functions.	Culture is a pattern of shared values and basic assumptions which perform functions concerning external adaptation and internal integration.
Symbolism	The organization is a human system which expresses complex patterns of symbolic actions.	Culture is a pattern of socially constructed symbols and meanings.

Rationalism

The rationalist view sees organizational culture as a means or tool for effectively achieving a given objective (Peters and Waterman, 1982; Deal and Kennedy, 1982; Kilmann et al., 1985). Within a rationalist perspective culture is typically defined by several variables, all synonymous with the notion of values. Hence: 'Culture can be defined as the shared philosophies, ideologies, values, assumptions, beliefs, expectations, attitudes and normals that knit a community together' (Kilmann et al., 1985:5). Rationalism is often an extreme variant of an integration paradigm in that subcultures are assumed to be in conflict with efficient fulfillment of the organization's common objective.

Since the organizational culture has the character of one or several variables, organizational culture can be separated from other organizational variables and affect the organization's efficiency and performance. Kilmann et al. (1985), for example, discusses the cultural variables' influence on the organization. This influence is based on:

1. The culture's *direction,* discussed in relation to the organization's formal objective.
2. The culture's *impact:* 'the degree to which culture is widespread or shared among the members of the group' (Kilmann et al., 1985:4).
3. The culture's *strength:* 'the level of pressure that a culture exerts on members in the organization' (Kilmann et al., 1985:4).

Hence, a rationalist perspective emphasizes classic assumptions concerning efficiency within a means-ends rationality. When transferred to the concept of culture rationalism focuses on the calculated elaboration of organizational values, which are analyzed and evaluated in terms of their contribution to predefined organizational goal-achievement.

Functionalism

A second important perspective in the debate on organizational culture is functionalism, which derives from classical anthropology and organizational systems theory and raises questions of how social systems continue to survive and adapt (Parsons, 1951). Functionalism perceives organizations as natural systems, which primarily pursue organizational survival by carrying out necessary functions. Organizational culture is viewed according to its contribution to organizational survival.

Cultural analysis thus asks the questions: 'What does culture do, what function does it have?', 'How does it arise, evolve and change?' (Schein, 1985a:49). The functionalist perspective discussed here specifies that in order to survive the organization must be able to adapt to the external environments and to integrate its internal processes. Thus, what organizational culture does is to solve the organizational members' basic problems of external adaptation and internal integration as they develop and learn values and assumptions according to this problem-solving. The specification of culture's functions allows the functionalist perspective to analyze the origin and contents of the organizational culture related to the various functions and diagnose how the organizational culture contributes to organizational survival.

Functionalism focuses on the processes by which values and assumptions become shared among organizational members and the formation of group identity, but does not reject that organizational subcultures may develop due to specific circumstances in the organization.

Symbolism

Symbolism is a third perspective for understanding organizational culture. It is less precise than rationalism and functionalism and sometimes appears only to share with them the concept of the symbol (Pondy et al., 1983; Geertz, 1973; Frost et al., 1985). The symbolist orientation perceives organizations as human systems which express patterns of symbolic actions. Thus, the fundamental question asked by symbolism is: what is the meaning of the organization to its members? Actions do not take place according to mechanical cause-effect relations or the need for organizational survival, but rather, due to social constructs regarding the meanings of various acts.

The organizational reality thus becomes a symbolic construction where the physical world is converted into a symbolic universe (Cassirer, 1944): 'The central message of symbolism is that humans act (symbolically), organisms behave' (Pondy et al., 1983:22). As such, the symbolic perspective assumes that organizational members are devoted to assign meaning - and indeed very often a meaningful order – to organizational behavior upon which they react. The anthropologist Geertz applies the text metaphor as an image for interpreting the organizational culture. Like the literary critic, the cultural analyst 'reads' the organization with the intention of crystallizing a pattern of meanings: 'social scientists should view and "read" social life as if it were a living document' (Pondy et al., 1983:223). The aim of interpreting organizational culture is thus to understand the meanings and symbols, as they are being created by the members of the organization.

From a symbolist perspective, subcultures are not necessarily including different limited parts of groups in the organization. Instead, subcultures can be viewed as competing patterns of interpretation where the same person will belong to a shared culture in some situations, and be part of a subculture in another.

Choice of Competing Perspectives

This book's subsequent theoretical and empirical discussion of organizational culture departs from the functionalist and symbolist perspectives.

Functionalism and Symbolism

The justification for this choice is that organizational culture theory is characterized by such diversity that we cannot speak of it as a 'normal science' (Kuhn, 1962). This diversity facilitates competition between different analytical perspectives. In this context to rely on only one of these cultural perspectives might lead to artificially neglecting alternative frameworks which could provide supplementary, or even more fruitful explanations. Hence, we have chosen to emphasize two of the most widely used perspectives on organizational culture: functionalism and symbolism. The main differences between functionalism and symbolism, which will be further elaborated in the following chapters, are shown in Table 1.2.

Table 1.2. Main Differences between Functionalism and Symbolism

	Functionalism	Symbolism
Key question	What are the functions of culture to organizational survival?	What are the meaning of the organization to the organizational members?
Key assumption	Culture develops when organizational members solve problems of external adaptation and internal integration.	Organizational members create meaning and define the organizational reality upon which they react.
Analytical result	A diagnosis of organizational culture and how it contributes to organizational survival.	An understanding of the symbols and meanings of the organizational culture and how they are created by the members of the organization.

Functionalism and symbolism can be viewed as attempts to elaborate the difference between culture as variable and as root metaphor. Functionalism stems from a variable perspective, although one which regards culture as several, very comprehensive variables which create a system. Symbolism, in contrast, emerges out of a metaphor perspective, even though it also attempts to distinguish different cultural phenomena from each other. It contains, however, a more concrete conceptual apparatus than Smircich's (1983a) distinction and is therefore more applicable to an empirical analysis.

The distinction between integration, differentiation and ambiguity cuts across these two perspectives, in that organizational culture in principle can be shared or divided within both functionalism and symbolism. The existence of subcultures is, rather, an empirical question both within functionalism and symbolism. In contrast, ambiguity conflicts with functionalism's demand for clarity and functionality, whereas the symbolic perspective more effectively integrates the members' polyvalent interpretations of the same symbols. Both functionalism and symbolism, however, are theoretically rooted in an integration concept, utilizing differentiation and ambiguity to pose critical questions at the empirical level.

Finally, we do not include the rationalist cultural perspective because it represents the least innovative approach to organizations. The rationalist perspective transfers the 'machine mind-set' to the domain of culture, thereby reducing the culture concept's development possibilities. The renewing and refreshing powers of the culture concept have in fact been based on an anti-rationalist rupture with the machine metaphor so predominant in organizational theory.

Empirical Field of Study

In the following chapters, the functionalist and the symbolic perspective will be elaborated theoretically and applied to the same empirical field. Thus, the two different ways of doing cultural analysis will be illustrated by empirical material originating from the same organizations, which hereby serve as illustrative cases. The empirical field of this book is a public bureaucracy within the Danish central administration. Within the overall organization, the ministry, we will concentrate on two of its four organizational units: a department and a directorate. The ministry is used as an illustrative case for elucidating different cultural perspectives. We have no intentions of elaborating two complete cultural studies on the ministry, but to develop and apply two perspectives for analyzing a specific organizational culture.

Choice of Focus

The ministry has been chosen as an illustrative case for several reasons. First, there is a need for empirical cultural analysis of bureaucratic organizations. Our understanding of bureaucracy has been dominated by a mechanistic bureaucratic theory or by political systems analysis, which lacks in-depth knowledge of the organization's everyday life (Morgan, 1986; Scott, 1992; Christensen, 1984). Public bureaucracies are not the kind of organizations which we normally think of when we discuss the culture concept. Neither Schein (1985a), Peters and Waterman (1982), Frost et al. (1985), Martin and Meyerson (1988) discuss the culture of public bureaucracies. On the contrary, the empirical examples of organizational culture have to a large extent focused on large and well known companies like Disney Land, IBM, 3M, Apple Computer, Scandinavian Airlines, all characterized by elaborate managerial attempts to create a shared organizational culture and a distinct image.

The organizations most resembling the central bureaucracy are hospitals (Sapienza, 1985), military organizations (Pondy, 1983), insurance companies (Smircich and Morgan, 1982), undertakers' shops (Barley, 1983), hospitals and local authorities (Czarniawska-Joerges, 1988; 1992) with the exception of Feldman (1989) who explicitly studies the paradoxical culture of the US Department of Energy. Several of these studies show that the culture of public bureaucracies has typically developed along much more subtle and tradition-bound paths, and only in recent years have public managers – if at all – started to reflect on their own organizational culture.

It is the argument of this book that the bureaucracy's colorful interpretations, absurdities and deep-rooted traditions have tended to be overlooked by the very simplified machine metaphor, leaving descriptions of bureaucratic culture to either claustrophobic Kafka-inspirations or to the classical, disillusioned spy-novel (Le Carré, Deighton in particular). A cultural perspective can help bring into focus these characteristics of bureaucratic organizations of which the ministry is a classic example. The organization is described in Appendix 1.

Furthermore, I was able to get access to the central bureaucracy, interacting directly with the political minister on a day to day basis. Obtaining such access is often difficult since the staff (especially within the department) tend to focus their attention on the needs of the minister (a political appointee) and because they are apprehensive about the press. I was able to overcome these reservations in large part.

Finally, the ministry's task situation will increasingly be characterizing public organizations in general in coming years, i.e. broad decentralization and attempts to develop new forms for influencing the societal sector areas. The ministry's situation is characterized by a need for defining a new task profile and adapting the old organization to changing tasks. This makes our study of the ministry a suitable case for illustrating the dynamics of organizational culture.

Empirical Material

The empirical material used in the case study is summarized in Appendix 2. It includes a vast number of interviews, along with observations of meeting activities. In addition, I have followed several concrete events and cases which occurred during the study, and consulted ministerial archives, reports, memos, etc. Finally, in order to obtain background knowledge for formulating the interview guide, I examined the organization's previous structure and task development, which has been documented in a long series of internal committees, reports and working papers. When collecting the data I guaranteed the interviewees anonymity and promised to restrict my usage of citations. In order to keep the identity of the ministry anonymous, the internal reports and papers are not listed in the bibliography. Also, the interview guides are not included as the questions posed typically related to the ministry's concrete task-area.

The cultural analyses based on functionalism and symbolism are drawing on the same empirical data. An important task in operationalizing the two perspectives, however, is to specify the kind of data they require and how these data should be utilized. Further specification of the data and the consequent methodological problems arising from its use are discussed in the application of the two perspectives.

Chapter 2
A Functionalist Perspective

A functionalist perspective views organizational culture in terms of the functions which culture carries out in the organization. First of all, such a perspective asks: what functions does culture fulfill in the organization? The functionalist perspective, as presented here, draws first of all upon the contributions by Edgar Schein (1985a; 1992). However, in several respects the use of a functionalist way of thinking is taken further in this chapter in order to apply the functionalist perspective to empirical analysis.

The Functions of Organizational Culture

The functionalist perspective on organizational culture is first of all based on Edgar Schein's contributions (1992; 1991; 1987; 1985a; 1985b; 1984). Schein is a dominant personality in the culture debate and his book *Organizational Culture and Leadership* (1985a; 1992) presents the most coherent and interesting presentation of a functionalist understanding of culture (see also Dyer, 1985; Louis, 1983). Schein is not a 'pure' functionalist. He has reservations and modifications regarding the functionalist view of totality and harmony.

It is the argument of this book, that the functionalist way of thinking affects the concept of organizational culture on different levels of abstraction. Functionalism both provides a functional explanation of the existence of organizational culture and rests the empirical analysis of organizational culture on its specific functions within the organization.

The Functional Existence of Culture

The functionalist perspective's theoretical point of departure is that organizations – like biological organisms – must successfully perform several vital functions in order to survive. Hereby, the basic theoretical assumption within functionalism states organizational survival as the key in understanding organizations (Scott, 1992; Parsons, 1951).

The model assumes that the social unit, in our case the organization, has certain needs of requirements that must be met if it is to persist in its present form. The specific structures that constitute the organization are analyzed in terms of the needs they meet, the functions they perform in ensuring the survival of the system (Scott, 1992:55).

In general organizational theory Parsons has used a functionalist way of thinking by claiming four basic functions that all social systems must perform if they are to persist:

Adaptation:	The problem of acquiring sufficient resources.
Goal Attainment:	The problem of setting and implementing goals.
Integration:	The problem of maintaining solidarity or coordination among the subunits of the system.
Latency:	The problems of creating, preserving, and transmitting the distinctive culture and values (in Scott, 1992:69).

These functions address the overall existence of organizations and, thus, do not distinguish between the functions of the formal structure and the organizational culture.

Based on the same claim of functional requirements necessary to all social units, the functionalist perspective as outlined by Schein (1985a; 1992), states that in order to survive, any organization must resolve two fundamental problems: (1) survival in and adaptation to the external environment; (2) integration of its internal processes to ensure the capacity to continue to survive and adapt (Schein, 1992:51).

The organizational culture is the product of the group's collective process of learning and problem solving in these efforts to survive. Organizational culture is a means of fostering integration in the organization – a consensus-creating 'glue' – which has decisive influence on ensuring the organization's survival. However, culture also evolves via the organization's necessary adaptation to external conditions.

Thus, within the functionalist perspective organizational culture is analyzed according to the functions which culture takes on within the organization and is defined by Schein as:

> A pattern of shared basic assumptions that the group has learned as it solved its problems of external adaptation and internal integration, that has worked well enough to be considered valid and, therefore, to be taught to new members as the correct way to perceive, think and feel in relation to those problems (Schein, 1992:12).

Even though the notion of organizational culture is conceived in terms of organizational uniqueness, the culture evolves as a solution to certain universal problems which all organizations must solve in order to survive. Without a functional means of dealing with these fundamental problems of survival, in terms of external adaptation and internal integration, the organization will cease to persist.

The Functional Explanation of Culture

Following a functionalist way of arguing, the emergence and existence of organizational culture is explained in terms of the functions it performs to internal integration and external adaptation, rather than in terms of its meaning to the members of the organization.

Within functionalism, the existence of different elements in organizations is explained by the functions which the elements execute in relation to the organization's survival. As Scott (1992:55) explains, 'the existence of an element is explained in terms of its consequences – the function it performs – rather than by reference to its origins'. If the system element is dysfunctional in relation to organizational survival, the element either ceases to exist, or the organization stops operating. Thus, if the organizational culture develops assumptions in relation to problems of internal integration which imply organizational fragmentation and severe conflicts, the cultural assumptions will either change, or the organization will disintegrate – and at its most extreme cease to survive.

Used here, functionalism has its roots in 'the paradigm of social facts' (Ritzer, 1975; Burrell and Morgan, 1979). Social phenomena are called social facts because they are treated as things (Durkheim, 1972), which are external in relation to the individual's understanding of them and can therefore exert pressure on the individual. Social structures and social institutions are factual, measurable, and delimited phenomena which – independent of the organization members' interpretations – can be functional or dysfunctional in relation to organizational survival (Ritzer, 1975; Burrell and Morgan, 1979).

The Functions of Organizational Culture

In the further specification of the functions of culture Schein discusses, from a dynamic perspective, the problems that occur in the development in new organizations:

> To specify these functions more completely, we must list, from an evolutionary perspective, the issues that a group or an organization faces from its origin through to its status of maturity and decline (Schein, 1985a:50).

And in the later version of the book this dynamic cycle is explained as:

The issues or problems of external adaptation and survival basically specify the coping cycle that any system must be able to maintain in relation to its changing environment (Schein, 1992:52).

Based on the overall distinction between problems in relation to external adaption and internal integration, the organizational culture develops when members of organizations must cope with a number of more specific problems in the process of getting organizations to work. These more specific functions of the organizational culture are summarized in Table 2.1.

Table 2.1. The Problem of Internal Integration and External Adaptation where Culture Develops and Functions

External adaptation	Internal integration
Mission and strategy	Common language and conceptual categories
Goals	Group boundaries and criteria for inclusion and exclusion
Means	Power and status
Measurement	Intimacy, friendship and love
Correction	Rewards and punishment
	Ideology and religion

(After Schein 1992:52, 70, 71.)

The cultural functions are the basis for the 'survival-learning process' that generations of organizational members go through and constitute the areas where the organizational culture is especially visible. In particular culture is developed in relation to 'mission and strategy', 'group boundaries', 'power and status', etc. because these are critical functions in the organization which are needed to insure the organization's survival and, thus, problems that the organizational members must address and discuss in the organization's development.

As shown in Table 2.1 Schein defines eleven problem areas within external adaptation and internal integration in relation to which culture's functions are involved. However, in this book the cultural functions are further classified and reformulated from a general organizational analysis of the empirical field, here an actual organization, the department within a Danish government ministry, whose culture is analyzed in the following chapter. The general division into external adaptation and internal integration is maintained, but in opposition to Schein's claim for universal functions that any organizational must perform, this book takes exception to Schein's assertion that the survival problems defined are all equally relevant for any social systems. Based on the insights from contingency theory

(Mintzberg, 1979) it is highly likely that also the functions of organizational culture will depend, among other things, on the concrete task-environment and the specific history of the organization. The concrete specification of cultural functions will be dealt with later in the operationalization of the functionalist perspective in relation to the empirical analysis of the department.

No matter what the specific functions of culture within a concrete organization are, it is expected within functionalism that members of the organization most likely will share the assumptions of culture. Organizational culture is thus defined as a shared and collective property of the organization, namely:

> The process of culture formation is, in a sense, identical to the process of group formation i that the very essence of "groupness" or group identity, the shared patterns of thought, belief, feelings, and values that result from shared experience and common learning results in the pattern of shared assumptions... without a group there can be no culture and without some shared assumptions, some minimal degree of culture, we are really talking only about an aggregate of people, not a group (Schein, 1992:52).

No matter which functions of internal integration and external adaptation dominate the development of cultural assumptions, the members of the organization will over time share a common view of the world, given they have the opportunity to interact and exchange organizational experience.

The Levels of Culture

An understanding of the organizational culture is necessary for 'an understanding of the mysterious and seemingly irrational things that go on in human systems' (Schein, 1985a:4). Culture is a common, collective property of the organization, which is difficult and cumbersome to understand if one begins with the organization's confused and complex surface.

Three Levels of Culture

In its most general definition organizational culture consists of the pattern of basic assumptions, which define the way in which members of the organization are to perceive, think and feel in relation to the problems of internal integration and external adaptation. But the organizational culture in its full richness is analyzed from three different analytical levels: (1) artifacts, (2) values, and (3) basic assumptions. The basic assumptions are the deeper, fundamental features of the organizational culture, taken for

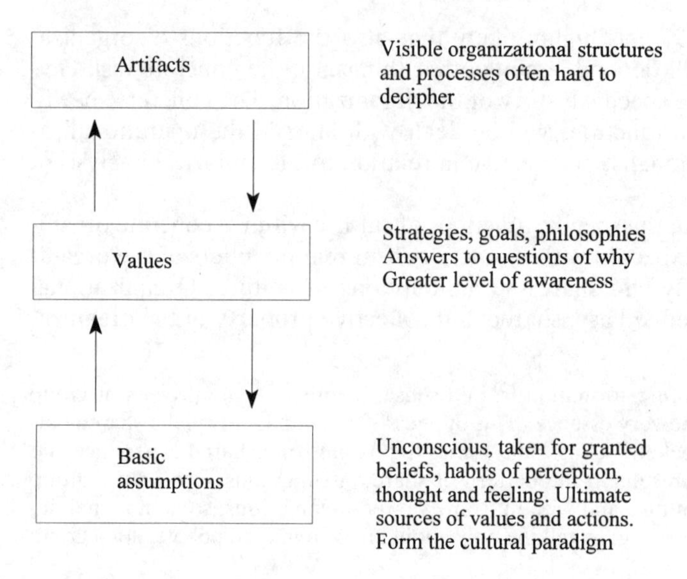

Figure 2.1. Levels of Culture and their Interaction

granted by the members of the organization, whereas values and artifacts are the organizational culture's more conscious, surface manifestations, operating at a greater level of awareness.

Thus, culture lies at the bottom of the organization, and can be discovered only with a special methodological net: a depth probing analysis which moves layer by layer down through the different cultural levels of the organization.

The three levels of culture: artifacts, values, and basic assumptions, and their internal relationship are illustrated in Figure 2.1.

Artifacts

In Schein's work artifacts are defined as:

At the surface we have the level of artifacts, which includes all the phenomena that one sees, hears, and feels when one encounters a new group with an unfamiliar culture. Artifacts would include the visible products of the group such as the architecture of its physical environments, its language, its technology and products, its artistic creations, and its style as embodied in clothing, manners of address, emotional displays, myths and stories told about the organization, published lists of values, observable rituals and ceremonies and so on... this level also includes the visible behavior of the group and the organizational processes into which such behavior is made routine, written and spoken language, artistic production and the overt behavior of its members (Schein, 1992:17).

Table 2.2. The 'Artifact' Level in Functionalist Culture Analysis

1. Physical Manifestations
   a) Architecture and interior arrangements
   b) Physical space and office design
   c) Decoration of hallways and conference rooms
   d) Dress
   e) Attendance
2. Language
   a) Sound and noice
   b) Modes of speaking
   c) Special expressions
   d) Slogans
3. Stories
   a) Minor stories from everyday life
   b) Stories of key events
   c) Tales of "the good old days"
4. Technology
   a) Materials
   b) Operations
   c) Knowledge
5. Visible Traditions
   a) Social traditions
   b) Leadership traditions
   c) Work traditions

Artifacts are characterized as 'visible but hard to decipher' (Schein, 1992:17). The organizational culture's artifacts create a multiple and confusing surface which leaves an immediate impression of the culture and typically appeals to prejudices and stereotypes. There is thus a considerable need to systematize the artifact level, both in order to avoid losing oneself in detail, and to avoid overgeneralized labelling of the cultural surface manifestations.

In the body of cultural theory several attempts to operationalize the level of artifacts have been made (Martin, 1993; Pedersen and Sørensen, 1989; Hofstede et al., 1990). Drawing upon these efforts, the artifact level is classified into five different analytical categories. These include various visible and audible cultural features as listed in Table 2.2.

The artefact level comprises visible and audible behavioral patterns among the members of the organization as well as a number of physical and technological features of the organization. In contrast to the level 'values', the study of artifacts requires immediate observation of the members' behavior.

Values

In contrast, values are seen by Schein as:

> All group learning ultimately reflects someone's original values, someone's sense of what ought to be as distinct from what is. When a group is first created or when it faces a new task, issue, or problem, the first solution proposed to deal with it reflects some individual's own assumption about what is right and what is wrong, what will work or not work... Therefore, whatever is proposed can only have the status of a value from the point of view of the group... until the group has taken some joint action and its members have together observed the outcome of that action, there is not as yet a shared basis for determining what is factual and real (Schein, 1992:19).

Values have a higher level of consciousness than basic assumptions, because they are not accepted as the natural reality and can be made the object of discussion. Thus, the values of the organizational culture have a normative character. They consist of what the organization's members say during and about situations, and not necessarily what they do in situations where these values ought to be operating. Values are articulate statements answering questions of 'why' and are therefore often the object of discussion. Used here, values will be defined as the premises used by the organization's members in classifying situations and actions in the organization as either desirable or undesirable.

Schein emphasizes the founder/leader's decisive significance in formulating new values for affecting and changing the existing culture. In some organizations the organizational values are formulated in a shared company mission, like the seven corporate identity components from the Danish company Bang & Olufsen operating in consumer electronics which integrate values in product design and organizing:

1. *Authenticity*. It is the company's aim to manufacture products, which ensure faithful reproduction of programme material.
2. *Autovisuality*. The company's products must provide for immediate understanding of their capabilities and manner of operation.
3. *Credibility*. We must constantly strive towards establishing confidence in the company, its actions and dealings and in its products.
4. *Domesticity*. The products are designed for the use by people in the home. They must be problem-free and easy to operate – even though they are technically advanced.

5. *Essentiality*. The products must be concept-bearing. Design should be focused on the essentials of the concept.
6. *Individuality*. Bang & Olufsen have chosen individuality as an alternative to the mass-producing giants of the trade.
7. *Inventiveness*. Product development and other tasks must be carried out with the aid of inventiveness. New approaches to solving practical tasks should characterize the company and its products.

In many organizations, however, values are seldom formulated as explicit declarations of guiding values, statements or as a mission for the individual organization. At best, the leadership or management formulates a few general values (e.g. two of four general values from Danfoss, another large Danish company being 'Danfoss is created by people', 'Danfoss cares for the environment') to which the organization is expected to adapt without friction and implement in various concrete situations.

Schein states that the analysis of the level 'values' results in a listing of values. The list seldom leads directly to the basic assumptions, however:

> Even after we have listed and articulated the major values of an organization, we still may fell that we are dealing only with a list that does not quite hang together. Often such lists of values are not patterned, sometimes they are even mutually contradictory, sometimes they are incongruent with observed behavior (Schein, 1985a:17).

And this notion is further elaborated:

> Large areas of behavior are often left unexplained, leaving us with a feeling that we understand a piece of the culture but still do not have the culture as such in hand. To get at that deeper level of understanding, to decipher the pattern, and to predict future behavior correctly, we have to understand more fully the category of basic assumptions (Schein, 1992:21).

Basic Assumptions

The basic assumptions, however, are the invisible and

> implicit assumptions that actually guide behavior, that tell group members how to perceive, think about, and feel about things (Schein, 1992:22).
> Basic assumptions, in the sense in which I want to define that concept, have become so taken for granted that one finds little variation within a cultural unit. In fact, if a basic assumptions is strongly held in a group, members will find behavior based on any other premise inconceivable (Schein, 1992:21-22).

The special patterns of basic assumptions which the organizational culture's members have evolved create the culture's core (paradigm). Hereby, the ultimate goal in devising an analytical classification of artifacts and values is to decipher the cultural paradigm: the pattern of basic assumptions.

Deciphering the cultural paradigm implies an analytical break with artifacts and values because the analyst must go behind the overtly visible or audible cultural features and attempt to dig out the deepest analytical strata which determine what the culture's members in fact do. In contrast to artifacts and values, the pattern of basic assumptions is not linked to the culture's specific function areas. The basic assumptions create their own paradigm which generates a coherence between the apparently isolated and confusing artifacts and values.

Using a comprehensive anthropological investigation of American cultures (Kluckholm and Strodtbeck, 1961), Schein (1992:94) has formulated the six basic assumptions from which cultural paradigms are created. These are listed in Table 2.3.

The contents of each basic assumption is further elaborated by Schein using several different social science typologies. For example, Schein discusses the basic assumption about reality and truth from various levels of reality like external physical reality, social reality, and individual reality, as well as he distinguishes between different kinds of truth, drawing upon the work of Max Weber. Thus, a full-scale analysis of the basic assumptions according to Schein's classification is a tremendous task, demanding a lot of substantial insights into how the members of the organization think, perceive and feel.

In addition, Schein does not provide us with a full-scale case study using his own model. He instead formulates far more concrete basic assumptions such as the basic assumptions operating inside the Multi Company:

'Multi Company' (after Schein, 1985a:110):

1. Truth comes ultimately from older, wiser and better educated and more experienced members.
2. Individual members are capable of and willing to give commitment and loyalty to the organization.
3. Relationships are basically hierarchical (lineal), but work/task space is clearly compartmentalized and allocated to members as their own niche or turf to manage and own.
4. Members of the organization are a family who will take care of each other.

Instead of trying to make his theoretical definitions of culture's basic assumptions more precise, Schein's results are 'imitated' in the subsequent analysis. Here we employ Schein's five basic assumptions as a guide. Yet we still need to formulate these basic assumptions in the individual culture's own words. It seems more useful to assume that the listing of the

Table 2.3. Basic Underlying Assumptions Around which Cultural Paradigms Form

1. *The Nature of Reality and Truth.* The shared assumptions that define what is real and what is not, what is a fact in the physical realm and the social realm, how truth is ultimately to be determined, and whether truth is 'revealed' or 'discovered'.
2. *The Nature of Time.* The shared assumptions that definethe basic concept of time in the group, how time is defined and measured, how many kinds of time there are, and the importance of time in the culture.
3. *The Nature of Space.* The shared assumptions about space and its distribution, how space is allocated and owned, the symbolic meaning of space around the person, the role of space in defining aspects of relationships such as degree of intimacy or definitions of privacy.
4. *The Nature of Human Nature.* The shared assumptions that define what it means to be human and what attributes are considered intrinsic or ultimate? Is human nature good, evil, or neutral? Are human beings perfectible or not?
5. *The Nature of Human Activity.* The shared assumptions that define what is the right thing for human beings to do in relating to their environments on the basis of the foregoing assumptions of reality and the nature of human nature. In oneSYMs basic orientation to life, what is the appropriate level of activity or passivity? At the organizational level, what is the relationship of the organization to its environments? What is work and what is play?
6. *The Nature of Human Relationships.* The shared assumptions that define what is the ultimate right way for people to relate to each other, to distribute power and love. Is life cooperative or competitive; individualistic, group collaborative, or communal? What is the appropriate psychological contract between employers and employees? Is authority ultimately based on traditional lineal authority, law or charisma? What are the basic assumptions about how conflict should be resolved and how decisions should be made?

(From Schein 1992: 95–96.)

basic assumptions does not have any universal validity, but can instead vary from one organization to another.

Internal Relations between the Levels of Culture

Schein assumes that the various levels of culture are in internal balance with each other. They have different degrees of visibility and analytical access, as both the levels of artefacts and values are surface manifestations of the culture's basic assumptions. The three cultural levels create a hierarchy of cultural elements in which the basic assumptions are the core of the culture which are so taken for granted. Yet when we do surface them, the cultural pattern suddenly clarifies and we begin to feel we really understand what is going on and why (Schein, 1985a:21).

The analytical goal is therefore – by detective work and commitment – to elaborate the harmonic and consistent core: the cultural paradigm, which is 'excavated' out of the organization by digging from strata to strata. The cultural paradigm is the 'core' of the organization's culture, which encapsulates and contains the other analytical levels.

The Cultural Paradigm

When the basic assumptions are listed, the question arises as to how they create a coherent cultural paradigm:

The final, and perhaps, most difficult aspect of the analysis of assumptions has to do with the degree to which they come to be interlocked into "paradigms" or coherent patterns (Schein, 1985a:109).

The degree of paradigm coherence seems to vary, such that strong organizational cultures typically possess strong connections among their basic assumptions, whereas weak cultures possess fragmented and inconsistent basic assumptions. The result of the cultural analysis can well be that there exists no coherent cultural paradigm. Schein summarizes the major task of culture analysis:

Unless we have searched for the pattern among the different underlying assumptions of a group and have attempted to identify the paradigm by which the members of a group perceive, think about and fell about, and judge situations and relationships, we cannot claim that we have described or understood the group's culture (Schein, 1985a:111).

In another study, Schein illustrates two examples of patterns of basic assumptions in the organizations he calls 'Multi' and 'Action'. The two examples of basic assumptions are depicted in Figure 2.2 and Figure 2.3. Here the basic assumptions are defined, and the relations between the individual assumptions are marked by arrows. An arrow between assumptions means that they support each other and enter into the establishment of a common, coherent cultural paradigm. In both 'Multi' and 'Action', the basic assumptions support each other.

When the cultural paradigm has been elaborated, it is possible to return and explain values and artifacts, which are easier to identify than the basic assumptions, but difficult to explain.

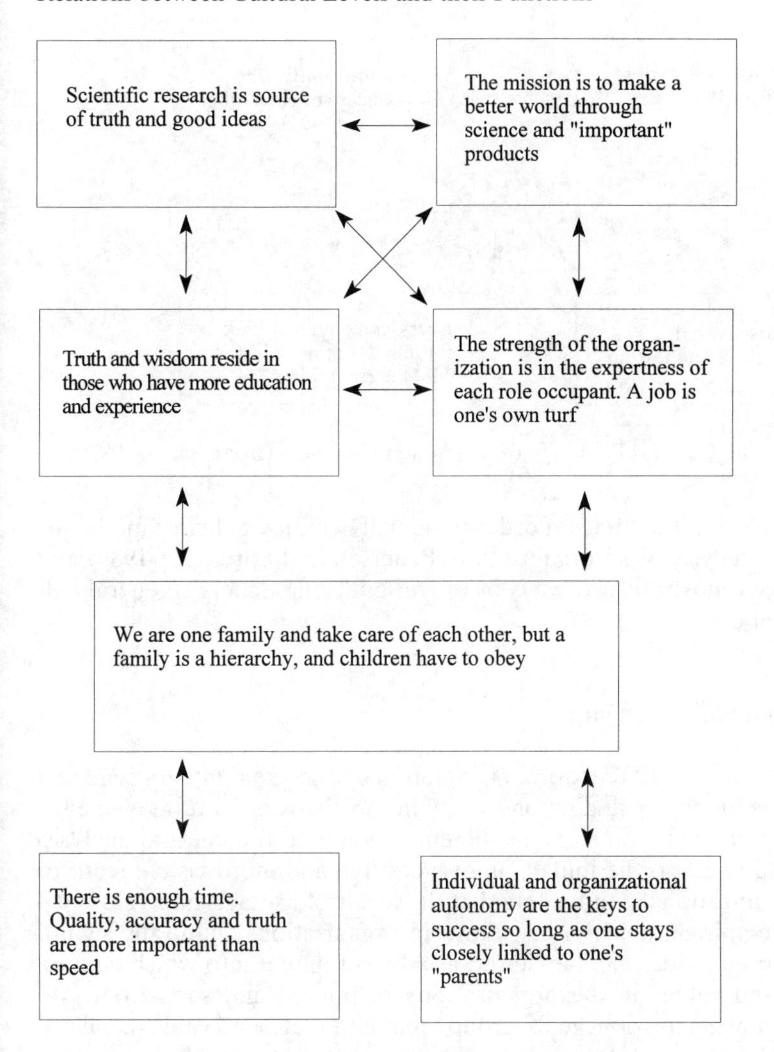

Figure 2.2. The Cultural Paradigm of the Multi Company (from Schein 1992:45)

Relations between Cultural Levels and their Functions

Despite Schein's many concepts of the functions and levels of organizational culture, there exists considerable leeway for formulating a more concrete functionalist analytical model. It is necessary to make a series of choices and make more precise the relations between culture's three ana-

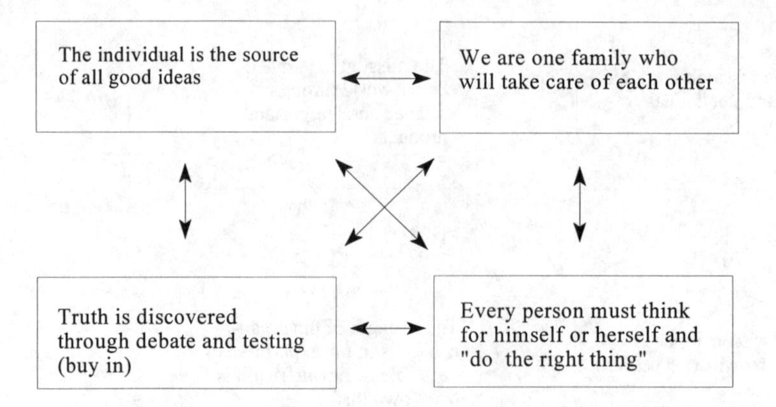

Figure 2.3. The Cultural Paradigm of the Action Company (from Schein 1992:36)

lytical levels and functions in order to actually employ Schein's model for a cultural analysis of an organization. Pedersen and Sørensen (1989) and Dyer (1985) illustrate two ways of operationalizing Schein's general culture concepts.

Sorting out Cultural Data

The functions related to external adaptation and internal integration are a kind of road map for finding one's way in the chaos of cultural elements. Thus, the functions can serve as the entry points to the cultural analysis, which help us grasp the immediately accessible and more visible features of the organizational culture found at the levels of artifacts and values.

In the empirical analysis of culture in organizations, culturally significant functional areas can be viewed as a broad funnel into which data on artifacts and values in the organization are poured and sorted out into artifacts showing mission, goals, group boundaries, etc. and values concerning means, power and status, rewards and punishment, etc. The idea of this 'funnel model' is that it helps to map out the organizational culture in terms of the different functional areas:

> Instead of getting lost in the infinity of cultural phenomena, the researcher and the practioner can use such dynamic categories as a road map (Schein, 1985a:49).

However, the basic assumptions denote an analytical break from the visible and articulate features of each functional area. Discovering the culture's basic assumptions presupposes an analysis of the artifacts and values shared among the members of the organizational or social unit. But the basic assumptions themselves are of a much more fundamental character

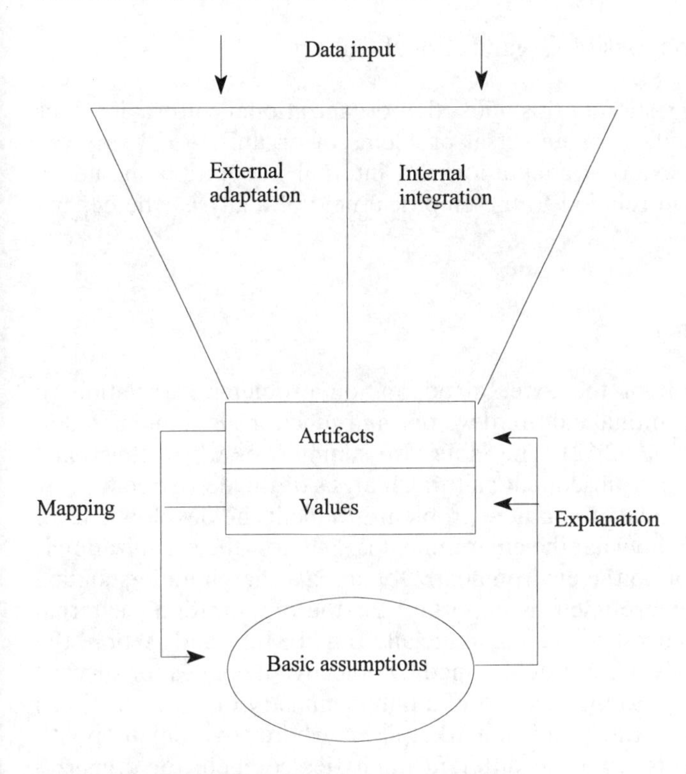

Figure 2.4. The Funnel Model

beyond the distinction into different functional areas. Therefore, the analysis of basic assumptions do not follow the distinction into functional areas of external adaptation and internal integration, but concern much more general assumptions of human nature, truth, and human relationships.

This analytical distinction between artifacts and values on the one hand, and basic assumptions on the other is shown in the model of a functionalist funnel, which is illustrated in Figure 2.4.

The functionalist cultural model in Figure 2.4 is called a funnel, because it functions as an analytical funnel into which the data describing artifacts and values are poured. Yet the model also illustrates that we are speaking of a circular process because artifacts and values are both the starting and the end points. At first they are used as the visible and conscious point of departure for an analytical mapping out of the cultural paradigm. Thereafter they can be deciphered and explained on the basis of knowledge of the cultural paradigm, and appear in the 'correct context' within the organizational culture.

The Specific Functions of Organizational Culture

Based on the suggestion of this book, that organizational culture develops according to specific, not universal problems of organizational survival, the functions of external adaptation and internal integration should be further specified in relation to the empirical field of analysis (the department).

External Adaptation

Schein's definition of the external adaptation problems in relation to which the organizational culture develops and functions is summarized in Table 2.4 (Schein, 1992:52). The table also summarizes which functional areas are used in the subsequent cultural analysis of the department.

In the operationalization a new problem is added: the development of consensus about who/what the environment is, and how the organization is situated in relation to the environment. Obtaining a shared understanding of the external environment is important for the organization's external adaptation; in contrast to the commercially based Multi and Action, the department's survival is not determined by objective demands for survival of the marketplace. Rather, as part of a public ministry the organizational survival depends on the 'political marketplace', where government, politicians and managers from the different ministries compete for organizational resources. Here, the department has evolved agreement as to who are its friends and enemies; who should be involved in the department's task solutions? Who among the relevant ministries and interest organizations are trustworthy? Who among the municipalities and local communities can be drawn upon?

In the concrete case of the department Schein's original 'mission and strategy' involves only a 'mission'. The mission primarily has the character of a calling which tells the organization's members who they are and why they exist. However, there exists no actual strategy, if we understand it as a conscious working out of a long-term strategy for the organization's survival. This lack of articulate strategy may be due to the perception that the core of the organization's calling or mission – to serve the minister and help to insure justice – is itself expected to insure future survival.

In the analysis of the department, goals are also excluded as independent problems of external adaptation. This remarkable lack of long-term and operational goals makes it difficult to measure the organization's results. The department does not formulate the exact criteria for measuring results. Therefore, the problems of 'measurement' have also been excluded as an area of external adaptation in the analysis of the department.

Table 2.4. Culture's External Adaptation Functions

Schein's (1992:52) Functional Areas	Operationalization in the Analysis of the Department
Mission and Strategy: Obtaining a shared understanding of a core mission, primary task, manifest and latant functions.	The External Environments: Obtaining a shared understanding of key actors in the environment, friends and enemies and the location of the organization.
Goals: Developing consensus on goals, as derived from the core mission.	Mission: Developing consensus on, who are we, why are we here, what are our strenghts and weaknesses.
Means: Developing consensus on the means to be used to attain the goals, such as the organization structure, division of labor, reward system and authority system.	Means: same
Measurement: Developing consensus on the criteria to be used in measuring how well the group is doing in fulfilling its goals, such as the information and control system.	
Correction: Developing consensus on the appropriate remedial or repair strategies to be used if goals are not being met.	Correction: Developing consensus on how means should be corrected, in case they no longer work according to their intent or are no longer politically acceptable.

Instead, the organization's members work within the much more limited horizon of the 'means'. Here, great emphasis is placed on fulfillment of form requirements – perhaps because it is extremely difficult to elaborate criteria for measuring results within a decentralized sector area with diffuse scientific standards. Thus, the lack of strategy and goals does not prevent the organization from a strong focus on the problems of stating and implementing means in the task-performance.

The lack of result measurements does not prevent greater attention being directed to correction of the applied means. Typically, the correction takes place because one has the feeling that the means do not work according to their intent. This may be because the political attention has changed which may necessitate correction of previous means, or because the resources for a certain type of activity dry up. No formal procedures for external feed-back and correction have been developed.

Internal Integration

The problems of internal integration, where the organizational culture must prove functional, are summarized in Table 2.5. Table 2.5, like the external adaptation functions, both inform Schein's definitions and the operationalization in the context of the department's conditions for organizational survival.

The first two problems of internal integration: common language and group boundaries are a prerequisite for being able to speak at all of internal integration in organizations; they are maintained in unchanged form. Power and status are also key problems in the department, where power is closely linked to the formal hierarchy. In contrast, intimacy, friendship and love, reward and punishment, and ideology and religion are not considered relevant in the analysis of the department, based on the data available.

The data does not allow us insight into intimacy and love, which of course does not exclude that there exist rules for dealing with them, or with sexual harassment, romances at Christmas parties and daily intimacies or intrigues. Reward and punishment are excluded because the reward mechanisms and criteria are tightly linked to power and status and an organizational pecking order. Reward and punishment are the sanction mechanisms used in distributing power and status, and therefore, in the department, do not have the character of an autonomous function. In the department, the material rewards of money, furnishings, and offices form an inseparable part of the organization's status system.

Finally, ideology and religion are excluded because in Schein's definition they entail 'according meaning to the inexplicable' (see Table 2.5). To explain the inexplicable is such a fundamental feature of organizational culture that it is not possible to restrict this to a simple ideology concept.

Instead, two new problems of internal integration have been added: leadership and standards, which reflect two basic features of the bureaucratic pyramid and the classic Weberian administrative tradition of public bureaucracies.

The many upward glances and references to leadership force one to put definition of leader roles as an independent problem area in the department. Leadership as a function area does not necessarily imply that there exists a functional leadership of the organization. Rather, it implies agreement as to what leadership is and what it is not.

Table 2.5. Culture's Internal Integration Functions

Schein's (1992:70-71) Functional Areas	Operationalization in the Analysis of the Department
Common Language and Conceptual Categories: If members cannot communicate with and understand each other, a group is impossible by definition.	same
Group Boundaries and Criteria for Recruitment and Exclusion: The group must be able to define itself. Who is in and who is out, and by what criteria does one determine membership.	same
Power and Status: Every organization must work out its pecking order, its criteria and rules for how one gets, maintains, and looses power: consensus in this area is crucial to help members manage feelings of aggression.	Power and Status: Every organization exhibits criteria for achieving, maintaining and loosing power. Jointly, the group must develop reward and punishment mechanisms for achieving and showing power and status.
Intimacy, Friendship and Love: Every organization must work out its rules of the game for peer relationships, for relationship between the sexes and for the manner in which openness and intimacy are to be handled in the context of managing the organizationSYMs tasks.	Leadership: Every organization must evolve ideas of what content of leadership is, what is rewarded, who exercizes power and the limits of leadership.
Reward and Punishment: Every group must know what its heroic and sinful behaviors are and must achieve consensus on what is a reward and what is a punishment.	Standards: The organization must evolve standards for equality and predictability, which create a framework for what tasks must be resolved and the way of doing them.
Ideology and Religion: Every organization, like every society, faces unexplainable and inexplicable events which must be given meaning so that members can respond to them and avoid the anxiety of dealing with the unexplainable and uncontrollable.	

Especially in a ministerial department, great emphasis is placed on developing uniform standards for resolving tasks, which, for example, might include the mode of procedure, priorities for time allocation in task resolution. The standards are linked to the administrative procedures and to the predictability of the organization's means of dealing with tasks.

The operationalization of external adaptation and internal integration informs the central problems which the department's organizational culture has evolved in relation to, and is herewith the key functions which the culture fulfills in ensuring the organization's survival.

A Functionalist Analytical Model: The Funnel

The operationalization of the functionalist culture perspective is summarized in Figure 2.5. Here, the funnel model is illustrated in relation to a few key problems of external adaptation and internal integration. However, the full scale implementation of the funnel model implies a cultural analysis of all the nine problem areas, which are part of culture's functions within the department.

The functionalist culture analysis has retained its original funnel form shown in Figure 2.4, but here the data input is divided into various function areas. At the same time Figure 2.5 illustrates that the ambition to map out the culture's basic assumptions is a means to evaluate whether or not the assumptions create a coherent cultural pattern.

Subcultures in Organizations

With its harmonic point of departure and the search for a shared cultural paradigm, functionalism does not search out subcultures in organizations, although subcultures are not empirically rejected. If subcultures exist, they are typically analyzed as 'several-cultural units-in-one', whereby different cultures in an organization are linked to different social groups in the organization. Also, within functionalism, subcultures are emphasized as an essential source of conflict in organizations.

The specific department, division or professional group evolves its own, autonomous culture (Martin and Siehl, 1983; Gregory, 1983; Raelin, 1991; Trice and Beyer, 1993). Thus, the structural differentiation into various functional task-areas (marketing, manufacturing, etc.) may provide the breeding ground in the development of subculture within the organization. It is probably less likely within a functionalist framework, that different subcultures develop according to the various functional areas of internal

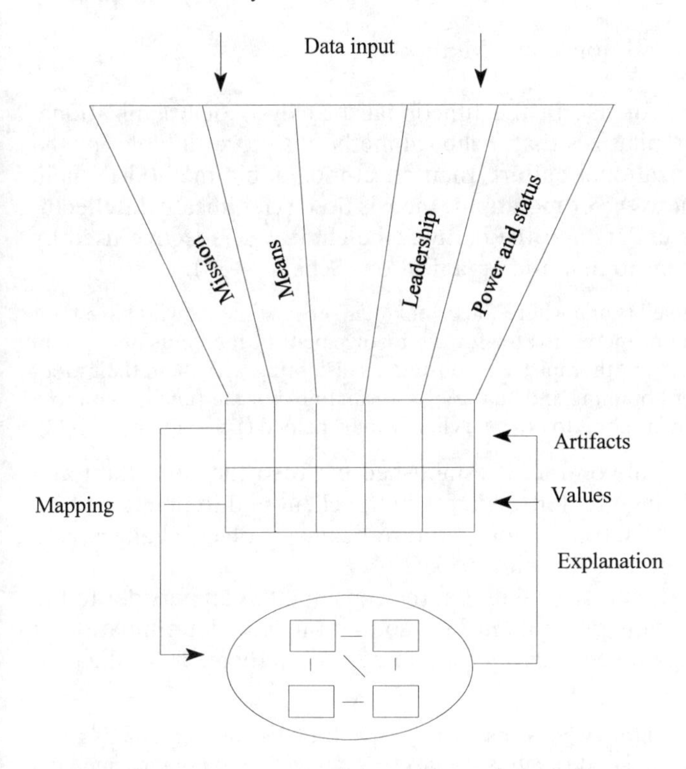

Figure 2.5. The Funnel Model Divided into Cultural Functions

integration and external adaptation, although the agreement on these issues may differ between the various social units of the organization.

Schein also notes that the existence of subcultures is closely connected to the developmental phase in which the organization finds itself. In the organization's initial growth phase, culture functions as a common source of identity and cohesion. Subsequent generational change, expansion and changes in the organizational structure create the basis for the emergence of subcultures in the mature organization, subcultures which can act as impediments to its internal integration and make the organization fail to reach its objectives (Schein, 1985a:Chapter 12). In situations, where values are consistently formulated by different groups in the organization one may question the degree to which different subcultures are cemented together within the organization, or whether the organization finds itself at the start of a learning process through which new values are being constructed.

A Clinical versus Ethnographic Method

In collecting data for use in the functionalist analysis of organizational culture, Schein emphasizes that a clinical method is more suitable for the analysis of organizational culture than an ethnographic method (Schein 1985a; 1987). Where the ethnographic view is used scientifically/intellectually and seeks to understand the culture, the clinical perspective used by consultants is meant to help the organization (Schein, 1987).

> "a clinical perspective" is one where the group members are clients who have their own interests as the prime motivator for the involvement of the "outsider", often labelled "consultant" or "therapist"... Consultants also bring with them their models and concepts for obtaining and analyzing information, but the function of those models is to provide insight into how the client can be helped (Schein, 1985a:21-22).

Here, a psychological contract is established between the consultant and the client, stimulating greater openness in the client and implying a more 'dynamic view of how things work, culture begins, evolves, changes, and sometimes disintegrates' (Schein, 1985a:22).

The clinical method is special in that the consultant as an outsider to the culture is working along with an insider, so that the final determination of the cultural paradigm becomes a joint effort between them. Thus, the consultant must

> find someone in the culture who is analytically capable of deciphering what is going on and who is motivated to do so. It is the insider's motivation to obtain some kind of help or clarity that makes this a "clinical" rather than an "ethnographic" approach (Schein, 1985a:114).

The clinical method presupposes that there is a need for a cultural analysis because the culture is dysfunctional in relation to the existing or future challenges.

In contrast to the ethnographic method, where organizations are observed passively and are left intact, organizational understanding in the clinical method is achieved via attempts to change the organization. The distinction between diagnosis and change of the organizational culture therefore has a primarily pedagogical purpose. From a clinical point of view, the diagnosis of culture can be interwoven with the introductory set of interventions. The validity of the culture diagnosis is here evaluated primarily according to its ability to predict actions and consequences in the organization.

Chapter 3
Functionalist Diagnosis of Organizational Culture

This empirical point of departure has been chosen in order to highlight the theoretical and methodological differences between the two theoretical perspectives rather than to show cultural differences between a number of organizations.

This chapter illustrates the functionalist funnel model by analyzing the organizational culture within one of the two ministerial organizations, the department. The chapter is not intended as a complete cultural analysis of the department. Rather, it provides an example of how such a cultural analysis could be accomplished. The functionalist funnel model will only be applied to one organization, as the concepts and the analytical methods are assumed to be the same within functionalism, no matter which specific organizational culture is being analyzed. Thus, adding further organizational data, is not assumed to redirect the analytical application of the functionalist perspective.

Instead of trying to elaborate a cursory analysis of all functional areas, the funnel model will be illustrated by taking two key problems of external adaptation and internal integration respectively, namely 'means' and 'power and status'. All those functions essential to the cultural analysis of a department have been discussed in Chapter 2.

In the cultural analysis, the same artifacts and values may be of importance in solving several tasks of external adaptation and internal integration. For example, office as a physical artifact has a cultural relevance in relation to both means and power and status. The distinct division into different 'offices' is the major tool in the task solution of the departement, just as the location (physical distance to the minister) and the task areas of the office are important determinants of power and status. In a total cultural analysis of artifacts and values, these only need to be described in detail the first time they appear in relation to problems of external adaptation and internal integration. The scope of a cultural description is therefore not necessarily so comprehensive as in the subsequent examples; it tends to diminish with the second and third problem area. The analysis of the artifacts' and values' specific function is maintained, however, through the entire cultural analysis.

Where no reference is given in the following chapters, quotations refer to statements made by members of the organization. By agreement with the organization, only a few illustrative statements are quoted.

Artifacts and Values in a Department

Means is a central problem area in the department because the maintenance and improvement of the existing means are viewed as prerequisites for getting the organization moving. Thus, the culture of the organization includes its members' consensus on issues like:

> One can have ambiguous goals, but one must agree on how to design, finance, build, and sell the good or service if anything is to happend at all. From the particular pattern of these agreements, not only the "style" of the organization but also the basic design of tasks, division of labor organization structure, reward and incentive systems, control systems, and the information systems emerge (Schein, 1992:58).

The organization's everyday life is to a great extent characterized by means. Specific tasks and cases constitute a criterion for distributing work assignments, for deciding the mode of work and for cooperation within the organization. In the adaptation to the external political environments, where isolated issues may easily cause tremendous political attention, means have a very distinct contents for the members of the department. Correctness and carefulness in each task solution are of significant importance, since slight details and misunderstandings may cause political disasters in an environment surveyed by political competitors, media and public control institutions. Thus, means is a key problem, facing the organizational culture, in the adaptation to the external political and bureaucratic environment.

In the tasks relating to the internal integration of the organization, the issue of power and status is of significant importance within the department. The problems of internal integration concerning power and status include primarily the organization's hierarchy or pecking order. The existence of a hierarchy raises several questions: What kinds of layers exist? How many are there? Who occupies the different positions in the hierarchy? What criteria are used by the organization's members to move up and down between levels? The department has a formal system of distributing power which divides the organization into vertical layers and creates stability and predictability in the members' everyday life and future. However, the organization is also characterized by an informal hierarchy based on differences between the various offices. This informal hierarchy is based on strong traditions in the department. Sometimes, the informal

Table 3.1. Artifacts and Values within Two Functional Areas of the Department's Organizational Culture

Artifacts	Means	Power and Status
Physical manifestations	Private offices Divisions of territory Uniformity Paper everywhere	Difference in: Office size Location Dress (formal/informal)
Language	'My case' 'Case-labels and -expressions' Indirect speech	Difference in: Speaking time 'Status' tasks Sections and chief of sections
Technology	Division of cases Delegation of cases Academic knowledge	Hierarchical stratification
Tradition	Fixed office division of labor	Status difference between legal sections and others
Stories	Change in work methods: from written to oral forms of work	The status and power of the head of department, minister as a shared favorite topic
Values	Cross-organizational collaboration in the department	Equality among the section
	Shared attitudes internally and toward the outside	All members are equally good at carrying out all tasks
	The best service to the minister	

hierarchy reinforces formal power differences while at other times it supersedes formal equality.

Table 3.1 summarizes the most essential artifacts and values in the department as they pertain to the two illustrative functional areas, where the organizational members have developed significant artifacts and values.

The Artifact Level: A Stratified Paper Pyramid

As shown in Table 3.1, the listening of the artifacts focuses on the analytical categories, defined in the previous chapter. However, only significant examples of artifacts are discussed here, indicating that the listening of artifacts may embrace a very wide range of observations.

Artifacts: Means

In terms of means, the organization resembles a classical bureaucracy: the paper pyramid where cases and dealing with cases are the primary tools for classifying and delegating the tasks which lie within the department's jurisdiction. The division of tasks is manifested via the office-based physical territories, where areas of competence and traditions draw boundaries between the individual territories. The acquired academic qualifications, despite changing work methods, have still retained their roots in the juridical tradition.

Thus, the physical artifacts reveal information about the department's division of labor. It is a key tool, when members of the organization define the means in the organizational task-performance, since all tasks are being handled from individual offices bundled together in larger sections according to predefined notions of how efficient task-performance should be accomplished. The division of labor includes eight section units organized within two divisions. It is illustrated by the organizational diagram in Appendix 1.

The division of labor among the sections of the department reaches all the way back to the ministry's reorganization before World War II, and several sections have traditions from earlier times. The principle for distributing tasks, labelled 'cases' has been adjusted in conjunction with the considerable legislative changes, but there was a continued respect for the historical traditions which the sections had been accustomed to from former times.

Within this overall division of labor, each of the professional staff members (called 'ACs') sits in his or her own office and has a private territory where the door can be closed to lock out the others. The territory is distributed among section units, which are typically created out of 7-9 smaller offices collected around a larger one. In some parts of the organization building it is clear which of the individual small offices belong together in a larger section unit. Signs orient the visitor to the section's location, the members go periodically from one office into another. However, in some cases, the offices are isolated in other buildings. Generally speaking, it is difficult to see which individual office belongs to which section, because they are all strongly resembling one another. All offices are equipped with a desk, telephone, typewriter and writing instruments as the dominant visible tools. In some offices, typically the larger ones, a dictaphone may be found, but no personal computers are to be seen. Papers lie about in most of the offices: orange-yellow file folders with white papers in them; bundles of white papers are piled up in the corner, small golden folders with black lettering and blue and green plastic binders, rubber bands in different colors in the corner of most desks.

These bundles of paper on the tables are referred to in all the sections as 'my' or 'our cases'. Some sections 'own' a type of case, other sections have ownership over other types of cases. By cases is meant for all the members the activities which every section carries out. Cases do not, however, stand alone as a prominent linguistic expression in the organization but are linked together with an area of jurisdiction. In addition the staff members have a rich rhetoric of cases, speaking constantly of case handling, speed of the case, case preparation, here and now cases, small cases, big cases, cases which run outside and inside, cases which must be tackled, cases which are put on hold or laid out, to go down into or dig deep into a case. Thus, the notion of the case is the key to the definition of tasks and how they should be proceeded in relation to the external environment.

Of course, many other expressions are used in the department. However, the hallways and the individual offices are often quiet in the department, leaving only the clicking sound of footsteps on the hard floor. The members are expressing themselves very economically when addressing one another; rather, they use short and indirect formulations with many words of hidden meanings leaving it an open question, what is actually said. Thus, the language is indirect and moderated, but presumably precise, if one is able to interpret the implicit code.

Together office and cases constitute the basis for the department's dominant 'operational technology' (Scott, 1992:244-245). The technology includes the division of papers into files and the distribution of files among the sections and individual staff members on the basis of previously defined areas of responsibility. The material used in classifying and processing cases in the organization is primarily the orange-yellow file folder, which contains the case's name, number, documents and any actions noted as they occur. Utilizing the department's technology requires special academic knowledge. Those in possession of such academic knowledge in the department are usually trained in Law. A *cand. jur.* degree gives them the ready knowledge, tools and mode of thinking which they employ to carry out their professional functions. However, one of the stories frequently told by the informants concerns changes in work methods. Previously, nearly all communication in the department was in writing; one worked alone, even though several staff members sat together in the same office and one kept to the nearest superior, who could be a special 'higher inspector'. The permanent undersecretary was somebody invisible. One had to muster up courage if one wanted to talk to him. Today, the department's work routine is considerably more oral. Most staff members do a little of everything and work much in ensemble even though they each have their respective areas of jurisdiction which they discuss with their head of section. The stories serve to remind one how much the department, despite everything, has changed, of how clever one has become and how good things are today. The department is a living, not a petrified, organism.

Artifacts: Power and Status

Within the department, power and status have generated a vertical, formalized rank order. The stratification is made visible in the department's physical artifacts, technology and traditions. In addition, the department is characterized by an informal hierarchy in which informal status differences overlap and cross sections occupying the same formal position. These differences are not physically visible, but can be heard via the differences in access to speaking time in certain situations, via gossip about status differences between assignments and via stories about 'good' and 'bad' sections.

By a first visit to the department, power and status differences are immediately visible in the physical manifestations; for example:

1. Differences in the size and furnishing of the offices, where the offices vary depending on the hierarchical level of their occupant; office area, number of windows, size of desk, quality of desk chair, the inclusion/exclusion of a separate meeting table, the presence of a carpet, the amount and quality of the additional furniture, etc.
2. The office's place within the hierarchy, in that some offices are located in the main building close to the minister, while others are further down the street. Here, the distance to the minister's office work as the measurement of power and status.
3. Dress styles differ between department heads and staff; the heads dress more formally (shirt and tie or suit) and wear more expensive suits than staff members.

Power and status differences are thus visible both within the department and in its relations with outsiders. These differences operate both as easily accessible information about on what level in the organization one finds oneself, and as a reward given when one moves up to a higher rank in the organization.

However, differences in power and status may also be heard in the department. For example: how much one speaks depends on power and status. At the executive meetings between the managers of the department and the minister, there are great differences in how much the various managers speak. It is only to a limited degree a function of how much the minister addresses the specific manager, just as the managers speak far more than the staff members. Furthermore, there is much talk of power and status among the organizational members themselves: who in the organization has power and status? Which are considered assignments with high status and low status? The heads talk of 'status differences' between the individual sections and the staff members talk considerably about how much status the individual heads have. Thus, power and status differences are a ongoing agenda in the organizational conversations.

Also, the standardized organizational structure serves as a constant reminder of differences in power and status. For the professional staff the organizational structure comprises a four-level hierarchy. The four levels create a one way ladder, where there is only one possible position at each level. The stratification operates so that promotion is possible only from lower to higher levels, which usually prevents any lateral movement. Stratification is maintained via the application of fixed salary scales, job descriptions, formal areas of responsibility, privileges (e.g. access to the minister), and placement in fixed routines. However, in spite of this standardized hierarchy, two legislative sections have had another and 'finer' formal position than the other sections being subordinated directly to the permanent undersecretary (i.e. the head of the department). The tradition has now been broken with the unification of the legislative offices into the legislative division, but has caused a lot of tension between the sections.

Such differences and tensions between the sections stimulate the circulation of stories about the various heads of sections of the department, stories which are extremely popular among staff members. Such 'head stories' deal with good and bad bosses and their power and status in various cases. The heads, in contrast, typically relate stories about how superiors have reacted in relation to their initiatives, emphasizing how much contact they have with their superiors. Everyone in the department tells stories about the minister. It is a common favorite subject in the department and provides important information about the current minister's views and special personal style.

The Value Level: Means

The values have been derived using interviews and conversations with employees in the department. The values are defined as the statements, made by the members of the organization, on how things ought to be. Thus, values have a strong normative character. However, in the department, there are mixed opinions about to which extent the values are actually realized in the department and how they should be realized. Thus, using Schein's distinction between normative values and beliefs, which represent statements about how things are, the members of the department share significant values, but hold different beliefs about the present state of affairs.

Cross-organizational Collaboration between Sections

One of the most widespread value orientations in the department is the need for cross-organizational collaboration between the various sections, located within each their division.

The members of the department all seek better cross-organizational collaboration and define it as an important goal for the organization, if it is going to improve it's task performance. Here, cross-organizational collaboration ought to include not only the formal collaboration between the various section units, but also the possibilities for informal conversation about everyday matters. The reason for this is that there is a tendency for staff members to keep to their own section and only speak with others in more formal situations (ACs' club meetings, civil servants' association, etc.).

Members also seek cross-organizational collaboration in task-and project teams. On a few occasions the department has attempted such collaboration and achieved good results, but the organizational members believe it has been complicated by problems of delegating tasks and of work pressures on individual persons. This is because the cross-organizational tasks have been viewed by certain sections as the responsibility of 'the persons and not of the sections'.

Thus, cross-organizational collaboration is considered an important value by the members of the organization, critical to the handling of an adequate task performance. However, under current conditions the organizational members emphasize the difficulties in accomplishing this collaboration, as 'cross-organizational contacts only create difficulties', and a special authority is required to 'make one's way' in such cross-organizational collaboration. Thus, the members hold the belief that collaboration is often cumbersome and difficult, and sometimes viewed as so illegitimate that it must be undertaken with extreme discretion.

Shared Attitudes

The value placed on having a shared attitude to matters concerning the department is especially strong among all organizational members: 'To create unity and shared attitudes – and avoid conflicts' is expressed as a strong wish and seen as a necessity, if the department is to 'go forward'. The value is most relevant in relation to the ministry's subordinate directorates and other ministries, as a shared attitude within the department makes these external relationships a lot more easy to cope with. According to the informants the relation to the directorate becomes full of problems and misunderstandings if the department does not have a uniform attitude. The heads of the sectional units also emphasize that the ministry operates far more effectively than other ministries when the department has a shared attitude, in this case preferably also including the directorate.

However, according to the informants shared attitudes are often lacking in everyday affairs, where the broad policy lines often vanish in disagreements between department's eight sections: 'People identify themselves with the work they do, which provokes a schism between the individual sections.' The individual sections have each become more clever, but now lack a 'common goal', 'a common conceptualization', or 'feeling of an *esprit de corps*' in the department. Thus, similar to the value of cross-organizational collaboration, the value of shared attitudes is given high priority when organizational members state how things ought to be within the organization, but still the value is not able to predict how the organizational members will behave in situations, where the value is expected to be operating.

Best Possible Service to the Minister

A third key value is the desire for the best possible service to the minister. Serving the minister ought to always entail setting aside other tasks and therefore complicating any priorities in carrying out assignments. This is because one never knows what will happen in the political arena. The views of how the minister attains the best possible service, however, are different in the department.

One view is that the department's task is to advise the minister in matters great and small, which is summarized in the formulation of 'being the minister's legal office'. In carrying out their tasks, emphasis is placed on security, careful consideration of cases, quick reactions and legislative expertise. The department interprets what the minister wants and in a qualified, loyal, efficient manner provides the minister with the required service. In order to function as an effective legal office for the minister, it is necessary to sense what the minister wants and be able to articulate things in the minister's 'spirit'. There is no time for 'guessing riddles' and one therefore must have a special talent for tuning into the minister's thoughts. It is therefore necessary to be involved, 'to have one's fingers into everything', so that the department can ensure that everything is as the minister wishes it to be.

A second point of view is that new means are required if the department is to carry out its obligations to the minister. According to this view, the most compelling need is to provide the minister with new ideas. Knowing how different political 'remedies' operate, the department ought to be able to establish an overall perspective and present different political options. The department ought to be able to point out to the minister the possibilities for doing things in a different way. The relation to the minister is here discussed in terms of being an 'active sparring partner'.

Thus, the value of the best possible service to the minister is also believed to operate in the department by all members of the organization. The value works as a superior guideline, but the organizational members hold different opinions about how the value is best implemented.

The Value Level: Power and Status

Equality between Sections

Differences in treatment can create jealousy, dissatisfaction and internal tension among the eight sections. Both heads and staff members therefore see equality among the sections as a central value for the department, building on strong traditions within academia. The informants explicitly state that lack of equality between sections may cause severe problems of collaboration and task performance.

Nevertheless, there are different beliefs as to what criteria exist for equality, and whether there is equality among the sections. Most managers describe status differences as differences in access to the minister, and as the individual sections' influence on the department's ongoing execution of tasks. In addition, the staff members also describe status differences in terms of how exciting the assignments are, how much the manager delegates to the staff members, and whether the manager is well liked. Moreover, they emphasize large status differences between the tradition-bound legislative sections and the newer economic-political sections which are 'up and coming' within the department.

However, regardless of which status differences are emphasized, there remains considerable agreement that 'equality between sections' ought to be a key value in the department.

Everyone is Equally Good at Carrying out Assignments

Both department heads and staff members express a value that everyone is equally good at carrying out their assignments. Hence, there is no need for 'experts' in the department. The value orientation is formulated in terms of the 'generalist tradition' within most public ministries, which assumes that all staff members possess the qualifications necessary to carry out any task. This value is underlined by the policy that criteria for hiring of department heads ought not to include any requirements for special expertise in the department's task area. A competent staff member, who otherwise fulfills the leadership criteria ought to be able to head any department.

Summary of the Value Level

The values express the members' explicit ideas of how the organization ought to appear when facing which means should be used in accomplishing goals and the criteria for the allocation of power and status. The values distinguish themselves in terms of how they are believed as being realized in the organization. Serving the minister is seen by all members as a key value, but there are differing views of how to achieve the 'right kind' of minister service. Cross-organizational collaboration and shared attitudes are emphasized as other important values, but both are formulated in the context of considerable dissatisfaction with the existing collaboration arrangements and internal attitudes. Both values in relation to power and status reflect a strong, shared emphasis on equality between sectional units as well as between the individual organizational members. However, there exist differences in relation to the specific criteria based on which equality should be obtained.

Basic Assumptions in the Department

In contrast to artifacts and values, the organizational culture's basic assumptions are not linked to distinct problem areas in the organizational survival. It is the deeper layer of assumptions about what is 'right' to do:

> Thus my assumptions about the right way to do things are more superficial than my assumptions about the right things to do (Schein, 1985a:85).

Description and analysis of artifacts and values produce an insight into the organizational culture and can be used to 'diagnose these deeper levels' (Schein, 1985a:85). The basic assumptions exist at a deeper analytical level and demand knowledge of the data which makes it possible to analyze the general dimensions of how members of organizations perceive human relations, truth and reality, human nature, etc. Thus, insight into the basic assumptions demands an independent use of data analyzed across the various functional areas.

The Method of the Analysis of Basic Assumptions

The basic assumptions presented here have been extracted from interviews and observations in the department as well as from impressions of informants working in subordinate directorates as to how the department operates. From the data and the foregoing analysis of artifacts and values, we can obtain insight into the members' underlying shared assumptions. It is not my purpose here to present an objective analysis of the members' basic assumptions which clearly and consistently appear from the data. Rather, the basic assumptions comprise my systematization of shared assumptions among the members of the department, assumptions which fulfill the following criteria:

1. The assumptions exist behind several different relations and situations and are thereby not specified according to distinct tasks or functional areas.
2. The assumptions form a shared framework for several of the espoused disagreements and conflicts which exist among the organization's members at the more superficial cultural levels, including both values and beliefs.
3. The assumptions are not coherently formulated by the members, but can appear in 'bits and pieces' in the interview or observation data.

The analysis of basic assumptions in the department focuses on six assumptions. Even though the analysis is formally separate from the individual functional areas, the choice of only two (illustrative) functional areas necessarily affects the analysis of the basic assumptions. A more comprehensive cultural analysis using additional problems of external adaptation and internal integration would provide material for a more profound analysis of the culture's basic assumptions.

Nobody Does it Better than We Do!

The members of the department assume that no one can carry out their tasks as well as they can. This is not because they never make mistakes, or because things never go wrong, but because there are no others capable of doing it better. 'It' refers to all the different activities which the members of the department carry out. 'Better' does not refer to an exact objective for the contents of the assignment but instead combines different dimensions of the assumption of infallibility.

The assumption contains a notion of quality, that 'ours' is one of higher technical expertise, better contents, and greater analytical quality than 'theirs'. The 'others' can do things in an interesting and different way, but in the last instance are unable to maintain the uniformly high level of quality and analytical scope the way 'we' can. At the same time, the tasks which the department carries out are so unique and specialized that it is not possible to transfer experiences to others, whether it is the current minister, who wants to have things done in a completely special way, or an assignment which demands special insight and experience.

The 'nobody does it better' assumption operates on several different organizational levels:

1. *The sectional level:* Even though there can be problems with a case in each section of the department there is no possibility of seeking advice from other sections. The other sections may be quite capable of carrying out their own tasks, but they do not have adequate competence in 'our section's area' nor the adequate expertise in 'our problems'. Hence, they are unable to do it better.
2. *The departmental level:* Neither the other directorates of the ministry, other ministries, municipalities or other sector organizations are able to do things better. They do not have the adequate experience with the political decision-making process and are unable to assess what is necessary for things 'not to go wrong'. Working directly under the minister, the department has become accustomed to assuring that things *'must'* be in order when they are presented to the minister, just as the time pressure connected to the political decision-making process has created an especially high degree of discipline within the department.

The Members of the Organization are at the Center!

The members have an assumption that they find themselves at the center of things. The assumption has the character of a local feeling in the department of being in the middle of everything, a feeling not bound to a specific time or place.

All relations emanate from the department to the directorates, municipalities, citizens and organizations. The members of the department locate themselves in 'the absolute center' of the sector domain, from whence signals and messages are diffused out 'into the system'. It is also in the department that the threads are again collected, whether this involves drafting legislation for the minister or collecting information to prepare a response to questions from the Parliament.

The department is also at the center of events. The events are the minister and the political life, because they constitute the point of departure for everything else which occurs outside the department. It is not specific tasks which are at the center of events, but the activities which draw momentary political attention. Only the department has the possibility to administer these activities because of its proximity and access to the political decision-making process.

Finally, the members locate themselves in the 'center of power' because they go each day, 'up and down through' the political power and become accustomed to dealing with power. The department is not viewed as having power itself, but has the unique privilege of being close to and directly subordinate to power. Via direct contact and the 'radiant glow' of power, the department obtains strength and authority over others in the system.

This Belongs to Us!

The department's members assume that they have a natural right to the 'things' with which they deal. Phenomena are viewed as things which can be separated and possessed, such as a concrete piece of territory or object. The living people at the end of a department's tasks, for example, are 'things' who can be labelled and manipulated; the directorates are things which locate themselves in specific organizational compartments; and tasks are things which can be classified, delegated and possessed by the organization's members.

This assumption is a prerequisite for the members asserting a natural right to ownership over things. It is not a juridical property right but a practical ownership, an assumption that a specific thing, territory or task 'belongs' to the department. The members dominate and have an authority-like relation to things.

The individual member of the organization occupies a private niche which must not be invaded by others. The tasks are sharply demarcated, they belong to the member and cannot be solved or taken over by others; just as a special expertise can belong to a specific individual and can therefore not be developed or acquired by others. The assumption is completely parallel at the sectional level, where each individual section has a special niche which other sections can neither invade, overtake nor imitate.

The department has 'ownership' over the minister in the sense that the department has the right to determine what the minister must know by the 'administrative path'. The department has exclusive access to direct ministerial contact and the sole possibility to determine who else within the ministry will have access to the minister. The (lower ranking) directorates, for example, have no right to contact the minister by themselves or to establish permanent niches in relation to the minister within the department's territory.

Finally, the department has ownership rights over its directorates. The directorates may be located far from the department's building and are subordinated and managed by the department. The directorates have neither the competence nor the prerequisites for keeping up with and adapting themselves to the political shifts, and are dependent on the department. The department's 'ownership' of a directorate is not a traditional relation between superior and subordinate, where the superior is responsible for guiding and overseeing the subordinate. Rather, the department can utilize the directorate in those situations where it is assumed to be suitable to avoid making use of the property right, i.e. in situations where things might go wrong for the directorate.

The assumption of a natural property relation has resulted in rules for dealing with individuals' and departments' rights to tasks, just as there have evolved rules for gaining access to the minister, the type of personal interaction demanded in the minister's presence, and the like. The assumption that ownership is 'natural' implies that it cannot be threatened, even though it is sometimes threatened by other ministries' intrusions into the department's jurisdiction or actual tasks.

The Organization's Members are Able and Ready to Passively Adapt Themselves!

Ability and will to adaptation are taken for granted in the department and encapsulate the members' assumption of how 'right people' behave. They are willing and able to adapt themselves to the conditions and expectations which they at a given time are subject to. Adaptation is assumed to be meaningful and harmonious, in the sense that the members adapt themselves to a given objective without frustration or irritation.

Adaptation is passive in the sense that the members adapt themselves to changing situations, without undergoing any profound personal change. They acquire patterns of behavior which are in accord with the new situation, but things still remain the same. The members are therefore always the same, even though they adapt themselves to rapidly changing conditions. The assumption is especially prominent in relation to:

1. *The minister:* The department's members share a common assumption that the department's *raison d'être* is a frictionless adaptation to the political attitudes and personal styles of ever-changing ministers. The department heads and staff members are reserved in presenting their own views to the minister, because they risk exceeding the bounds of the department's area of action, and because it may complicate adaptation to the subsequent minister.
2. *The hierarchy:* Hierarchical relations are the 'natural relations' in a department and are viewed as being the only possible way of organizing

> things. Competence and authority are taken for granted among superiors, just as it is considered natural to see one's own hard work thrown out, accepting it with 'head bowed' because a detail does not completely fit in at the given political moment.

At a more general level the assumption of the members' passive adaptation is an expression of the acceptance of fate, as a naturally given, external phenomenon which the members cannot change but must accept and to which they must reconcile themselves. Adaptation to the hierarchy is not a difficult choice to be made, but a natural, harmonious adaptation to existing conditions.

A consequence of adaptation is that the members react by distancing themselves from the contents of the activities in which they are involved. In principle, the members are ready to harmoniously adapt themselves to views of changing ministers, changing heads, changing tasks, etc., it is natural that they do not involve themselves in the actual contents but focus energies on the territory which they themselves control.

There is only One Truth, which can be Discovered from Within

The department's members have a basic assumption that there is only one truth. It will always be possible to discover the 'correct' thing to do, whether it involves dealing with a specific case, or presenting the minister's signals in relation to those outside the department. There exists no notion of several truths which can be 'equally correct'. The truth is not intimately linked to a certain method, but is discovered in all situations via a rational, reasoning process. Truth always exists as an absolute final goal but can be difficult to achieve.

The truth comes 'from within', i.e. it is discovered from within the organization. Schein emphasizes that in Multi:

> Truth comes ultimately from older, wiser, better-educated, and more experienced members (Schein, 1985a:110).

Schein describes a truth which is defined within the framework of the organization and according to the social process which takes place inside the organization.

In the same way truth is defined from within the department according to an internal rationality which is set via the social reality defined collectively by the organization's members. Superiors define truth for subordinates: the department defines the truth and the concrete reality for the sections and individual members of the organization. The members do not need to go out and seek the truth. It is assumed that truth can be found within the framework of the organization.

The Organization Members Constitute a Family which Works

The members have an assumption that the department is a small 'family unit' where everybody knows each other and where things work. In spite of the problems with the minister, in spite of things periodically 'going wrong', and in spite of internal disagreements, the organization works. The assumption that things in the department 'work' has two elements.

The members of the department function well together! They are not always in agreement and have different personal sympathies and antipathies, but they know each other and do not irritate each other. One seldom goes behind each other's back, and the managers place special emphasis on the fact that everyone in the department is satisfied. The members of the department constitute a small family, an island of patriarchical leadership which is both compassionate and determined. The members who, for one reason or another, do not fit into the department 'family' are never pushed out or sent off. As a rule they figure things out for themselves and leave of their own accord.

The department's handling of assignments works! Day after day the department produces legislative draft proposals, speeches, reports, and decisions demanded of it by the minister, citizens, organizations, and others. The department's handling of tasks is stable, firm, and very rarely are 'big things dropped on the floor'.

The Cultural Paradigm

The pattern of basic assumptions constitutes the department's cultural paradigm and is summarized in Figure 3.1. The paradigm derives from the contents of the individual assumptions.

The Core of the Cultural Paradigm

Figure 3.1 shows a consistent cultural paradigm with a strong, stable core centered on the assumption that 'nobody does it better than we do'. The department is strongly oriented toward its own significance and importance and views itself as being as close as possible to 'infallibility': nobody does it better than we do. These assumptions create a profile of an organi-

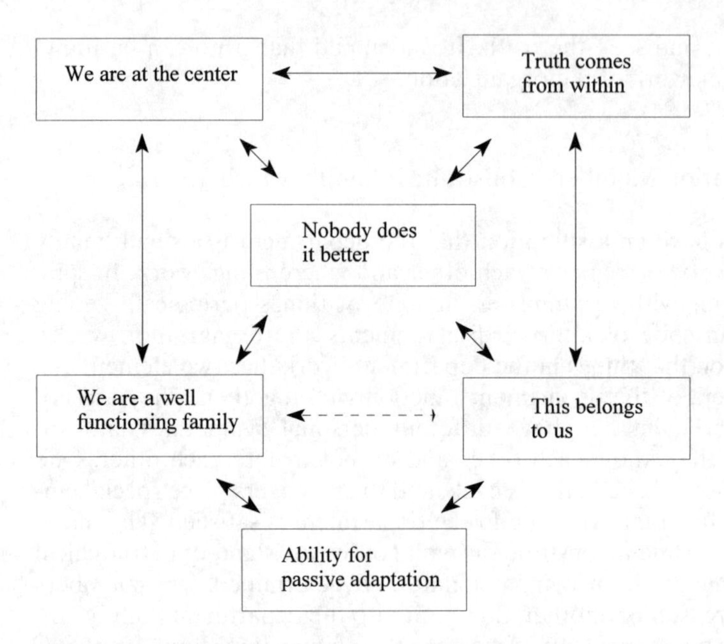

Figure 3.1. The Cultural Paradigm of the Department

zation which is clever at surviving without equal competitors: the department does not need to convince others that its execution of tasks is effective or sufficient. 'Others' will not be able to do it better and will seldom have the prerequisites for evaluating the contents of the solution. The members of the organization therefore have an extremely low incentive to interest themselves in others because the others are not perceived as being able to help the department carry out its work.

The assumption of 'nobody does it better' is tightly linked to the assumption of being 'in the center'. The center in which the department locates itself is defined in relation to others. The center is not a positive community focused on a special identity or special contents, but is negatively defined as something which others outside the department do not have. The assumption thus bears witness to an ethnocentrism, where a community exists by viewing the others as inferior and different, rather than being based on a shared substantial identity. The ethnocentrism means that the members of the department live parallel lives between community and individualism. The community among the members of the organization is an anonymous, negatively defined framework for the individual's everyday life devoid of positive contents. They are members of a community without having anything in common.

'We are at the center' is connected with the assumption that 'this belongs to us'. The assumption defines the members' natural area of action and specifies what kinds of relations are valid: the right of every section to defend its niche against other sections and the department's right to manage those matters which find themselves within this area of action. The assumption contains rules for specifying how individuals and sections are to carry out tasks and deal with problems, just as there are developed rules for access to the minister, forms of personal interaction with the minister, etc. The assumption that the right of property is natural ultimately implies that such a right cannot be fundamentally threatened, even though it suffers from interference by other ministries in the department's tasks and the directorate's attempts to create external contacts to the minister or encroach on the department's work.

These three basic assumptions create a consistent and strong axis in the department's culture in the sense that the contents of each of the basic assumptions is positively related to one another. The arrows between them are marked in boldface in Figure 3.1 in order to indicate a coherent cultural core in spite of the lack of direct connection between 'we are at the center' and 'this belongs to us'.

Consistency and Inconsistency of the Cultural Paradigm

The cultural paradigm's core of 'nobody does it better' is consistent with the internal assumption of truth and the assumption of familyness. The internally defined truth is linked to the organizational hierarchy where the highest placed staff member is closest to the truth and therefore owns the greatest amount of truth. Yet the assumption is also an indication that the members of the department, via their position in 'the absolute center', have better conditions than others for discovering the objective truth. Even though things could, in others' opinion, have been done differently, the problems with the existing management of tasks are never so great that the system fails to operate successfully. Thus, the assumption that 'the organization constitutes a family that works' establishes the preconditions for the department's experience of being 'the best' and viewing itself at the center of the universe. The family assumption also functions as an essential integration mechanism supporting the assumption of passive adaptation. Ministers and opinions come and go, but the department family remains!

A consequence of the assumption of passive adaptation is that the members distance themselves from the contents of the activities in which they are involved. The adaptation also results in an ends-means distortion, in which the adaptation is connected to the assumption that 'this belongs to us'. Frequent and rapid adaptation becomes a goal in itself, while the changing contents and the consequences of the concrete tasks dissolve and become but a means to a new adaptation. The members of the department become participants in an individual game of adaptation whose object is to adapt as quickly, as elegantly, and as efficiently as possible, whereas the contents and consequences do not count because they will soon change again anyway.

The only inconsistency in the cultural paradigm occurs between the 'familyness' assumption and 'this belongs to us'. This is because the natural right of ownership is typically based on the level of the individual sections. To the extent that the property rights are based on the organizational level, consistency is realized with the familyness assumption.

Because the cultural paradigm is consistent and stable, it is not necessarily functional in relation to the organization's external adaptation and internal integration. An evaluation of the cultural paradigm's functionality and consistency presupposes a return to values and artifacts.

Tracing Backwards from Basic Assumptions

Schein emphasizes that one can trace back from the basic assumptions and thereby 'explain' values and artifacts. Relations and connections between analytical levels can first be analyzed only after the basic assumptions have been elaborated. Schein does not discuss how this tracing back process is done, nor does he furnish a complete example of the relations between the three analytical levels.

Here the tracing back process will be illustrated in two phases. The first phase discusses the relations between basic assumptions and values. Values and basic assumptions are both cognitive elements (Festinger, 1957:9). In a wider sense, they constitute the knowledge possessed by the organization members themselves, their understanding of how phenomena relate to each other, and how things ought to be. The values comprise a normative and articulated self-understanding, whereas the assumptions are more profound ideas of how things really are.

Artifacts, in contrast, are immediate, tangible phenomena: they can be touched, observed or heard. Functionalism does not accord the artifacts with any autonomous cognitive contents, but stress that they are hard to decipher without having analyzed the deeper levels of the culture. The second phase, therefore, is to try and decipher how artifacts work within the organizational culture. Based on a functionalist way of thinking, the analysis will focus on which effects the artifacts have on the relationship between values and basic assumptions. A further analysis of the effects of the artifacts may explain their origin and, thus, separate the accidental and immediate occurrence of artifacts from a more profound analysis of their cultural importance.

However, both when tracing the relationships between values and basic assumptions and when analyzing the effects of the artifact level it is important to take into account the illustrative character of the analysis.

Relations between Basic Assumptions and Values

Schein does not specify which relations enter into the explanation between basic assumptions and values. However, given the functionalist assumption of consistency and harmony, a pure functionalism could presuppose relations which support and amplify each other. The analysis of the department, however, also contains values and assumptions which are not internally consistent. This is the case, for example, with the value 'shared attitude' and the assumption that 'members of the organization find themselves in the center'; equally inconsistent is the value 'equality of sections' and the assumption that 'this belongs to us'.

Similar to the analysis of the cultural paradigm, we can thus distinguish two types of relations between values and basic assumptions:

1. *Consistency:* The basic assumption accords with the value and supports the contents of the value. When this occurs the value's significance for the culture is reinforced.
2. *Inconsistency:* The basic assumption conflicts with the value, which means that the opposite basic assumption is well suited to it. In this case tensions may arise in the culture.

The relation between basic assumptions and values is set out on the basis of the contents of the two levels. The methodological problem is that the analysis of the elements in reality is determined by a center labelling of values and assumptions and may thus produce a self-fulfilling tracing back process on an all too fragile basis. One way of avoiding this self-fulfilling process is to undertake – after the analysis of levels – a special study of relations between values and assumptions, for example a study of the key functional domains. This exceeds the data base used here, however. A second possibility is a systematic argumentation for consistency and inconsistency. This can create the preconditions for an intersubjective evaluation of the results of analysis and help elucidate the unclear or ambiguous relations within the culture.

The argumentation takes its point of departure in the value level because the culture model's division into levels presumes that the assumptions underlie, and therefore explain values. The result is summarized in

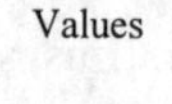

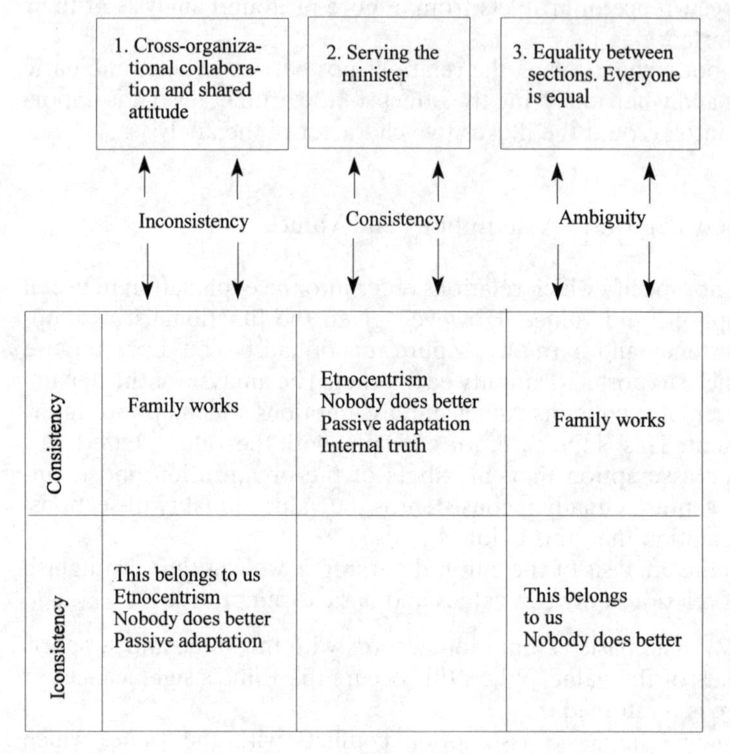

Figure 3.2. Relations between Values and Basic Assumptions

Figure 3.2, which shows that the values can group themselves into three categories characterized by different relations to the culture's basic assumptions, the categories being (1) Inconsistency, (2) Consistency and (3) Unclear, defined as the co-existence of both consistent and inconsistent relations. The argumentation behind the three categories of values is as follows.

Inconsistency between Values and Basic Assumptions

The assumption that 'this belongs to us' conflicts with 'cross-organizational collaboration' because the assumption is predicated on independent sectional units which have a natural 'ownership' of their own assignments. The 'nobody does it better' assumption is also inconsistent in relation to 'cross-organizational collaboration' because the individual sections are not assumed to have anything to learn from each other. The same reasoning is true of 'we are at the center'. All three relations change from the sectional level to the organizational level. The analysis reflects the fact that organization members tend to think in terms of sections as their point of reference. If they instead were to think in terms of the department, the assumptions would reinforce an internal collaboration and, thus, the internal integration of the department. At the same time, however, the external collaboration with subordinate directorates would be even more complicated because the department's assumptions of 'nobody does it better' and 'this belongs to us' would be transferred to the directorates.

The relations between the value shared attitude and the assumption of finding oneself at the center of things also generate tension because maintenance of 'we are at the center' is based on a community devoid of contents, defined in relation to others. A shared attitude risks that the members' ethnocentric community will break down and be replaced by differences of opinion and different relations to the periphery. Conversely, 'we are at the center' creates a vacuum, which shared attitude can fill, whereby the relation can become consistent. In the long run, 'we are at the center' can provide fertile ground for formulating a shared attitude, with the disadvantage that the attitude is defined primarily as a negative relation to the environment. The inconsistency between shared attitude and 'this belongs to us' parallels that of the value of 'cross-organizational', just as the agreement in relation to the 'familyness' assumption. Finally, the 'passive adaptation' assumption works against the desire to achieve shared attitude because passive adaptation is based on a notion that only a minister ought to have opinions. The inconsistency is thus not based on a contradiction between opinion and flexibility. The relation will therefore be changed along with the additional experience with assignments in which staff members must argue for specific opinions and uphold them.

Consistency between Values and Basic Assumptions

In contrast to the inconsistencies between the values of cross-organizational collaboration and shared attitudes and a number of basic assumptions, one basic assumption, the assumption of the familyness, is consistent with both values. The assumption enhances the goals of internal collaboration in that family coherence is based on things functioning in a collective. But the assumption also supports the value of shared attitudes in emphasizing the loyalty and determination among the members of the family. However, both values are dominated by inconsistencies in their relation to the level of basic assumptions.

In contrast to the two foregoing values, 'serving the minister' is the culture's normative core, being supported by several assumptions in the culture. The assumptions 'adaptation' and 'being in the center' create a clear basis for 'serving the minister'. The minister is the fixed star in the department's universe, the star from which other things emanate. In addition, the 'nobody does it better' assumption provides a basis for 'serving the minister's' especially honor-laden and elitist character, inasmuch as others can or will not be able to intrude on the department's monopoly over the minister. No assumption directly contradicts 'serving the minister', but giving too free reign to a strongly segmented assumption that 'this belongs to us' can come into conflict with the requirements of 'serving the minister'; specifically, the requirement that work be carried out in the general political interest.

Unclarity between Values and Basic Assumptions

The relationships between the values of equality and the cultural paradigm are characterized by unclarity, because of the combined existence of consistent and inconsistent relationships without a distinct dominance. Thus, in some areas the values are substantially supported by the basic assumptions, while in other areas they differ from the basic assumptions.

'Equality between sections' stands in explicit contrast to 'this belongs to us'. The control and desire to expand one's administrative territory does not accord with values of departmental equality. The assumption of 'nobody does it better' at the sectional level also points away from 'departmental equality' in the sense that sections with the highest, tradition-bound status cannot learn from other sections. The assumption of 'nobody does it better' thus affects the organization by helping to maintain the status quo. In contrast, the family assumption reinforces departmental equality inasmuch as it reaffirms the idea of belonging and reciprocity in the small department. Thus, the relationship between the value of equality and basic assumptions is characterized by unclarity, because there are simultaneously consistent and inconsistent relations.

The family assumption supports 'equality of tasks'. The argument that the relation between 'nobody does it better' and 'task equality' is parallel to 'departmental equality' is valid only at the individual level. Finally, the assumption that 'this belongs to us' also applies to the individual member's task niche, which can be neither invaded nor shared with others. 'This belongs to us' provides the ideological protection against 'task equality's' normative idea of flexible, frictionless change of tasks between equally qualified generalists.

A Mixed Culture

The organizational culture in the department is not uniform and harmonious in the sense that values are reinforced by the basic assumptions of the culture. The ways in which things ought to be are not always consistent with the perceptions and thoughts that the organizational members take for granted. Rather, the organizational culture of the department is mixed as the basic assumptions enter into several different relations at the value level. The basic assumptions are expected to have been developed through a long process of organizational learning and socialization and, thus, reflect the stable cultural characteristics with a strong historical origin, whereas values are in the process of being validated and reflect much more recent and conscious discussions in the organization about how things ought to be.

The culture's stable center of gravity is the value of minister service, which is supported by the greatest number of basic assumptions and helps foster the organization's internal integration. Here, there is consistency between the core assumptions of the cultural paradigm and the value of how the minister ought to be served, indicating stable historical assumptions about minister service and a strong organizational focus on the minister. However, the members of the organization differ in their opinions about how the best possible service to the minister should be implemented, parallel to recent discussions among bureaucrats on the future interaction between minister and department.

Several of the assumptions underlying 'serving the minister' are simultaneously conflicting with the values of 'shared attitude' and 'cross-organizational collaboration'. Both values are considered very important by the members of the organization and no doubt reflect an urgent need for improving the organizational task performance, which is rich in examples of the negative implications of organizational rivalry. These inconsistencies may express the need for external adaptation in relation to improved task performance to the extent that 'collaboration' and 'shared attitude' will be functional in relation to the organization's possibilities for external survival. But the cultural paradigm still holds a number of assumptions, typical of a self-centered bureaucracy with a strong emphasis on organizational territories and a low motivation to collaborate with anybody outside one's own turf. Thus, the inconsistencies between values and basic assumptions reflect a turning point in the cultural history of the organization in the sense that some of the key assumptions of the cultural paradigm will be challenged by the external pressure for a more collaborative behavior within the department.

However, these inconsistencies are somehow moderated by the assumption, 'We are a well functioning family'. The family assumption is the harmony-creating element in the culture because it ensures that the members do not give 'free reign' to the desire to control their own, central territory and to the feeling of being superior to others. Finally, in the domain of equality, the culture is characterized by an unclarity, where the family assumption on the one hand maintains ideals of equality while on the other hand being subverted in daily work by assumptions of 'ownership' of tasks and individuals' ideas of 'nobody does it better'.

The Effects of Artifacts in Relation to Values and Basic Assumptions

Based on the analysis of the relationships between values and basic assumptions, the functionalist diagnosis seeks to analyze how the more superficial artifacts work within the organizational culture.

The former analysis facilitates a distinction between the artifacts which are a part of the stable aspects of the organizational culture and those which may cause tensions and conflicts within the culture. Like the relation between values and basic assumptions, it is suggested that implications of the artifact level in the organizational culture contain two different possibilities, both focusing on the predefined functional need for internal integration.

1. The artifact level has here an integrating and, thus functional, effect in the organizational culture.
2. The artifact level has a conflict-creating and, thus dysfunctional, effect in the organizational culture.

Both of these effects of the artifact level are illustrated with examples from the data. The analysis of the artifact level's functionality can no doubt be further developed from a broader data base, also including the need for external adaptation. However, the artifacts listed in the previous analysis both in relation to 'means' and 'power and status' all show a strong emphasis on the internal integration. Our purpose here, however, will only be to offer a corrective to one of Schein's principle theses: that the artifact level, because of its immediately tangible character, can be analyzed using a functional approach when relating the effects of artifacts to values and assumptions. Table 3.2 contains examples of the different effects of the artifact level.

Table 3.2. The Effects of Artifacts in Relation to Values and Basic Assumptions

Artifact-effect	Relation between Values and Assumptions	
	Inconsistency	Consistency
Integration	1. Value-Assumption: Cross-organizational collaboration versus This belongs to us Artifact-effect: Office-territory, physical and technological factors legitimate a lack of cross-organizational collaboration	2. Value-Assumption: Serving theminister versus Passive adaptation Artifact-effect: Indirect speechmakes possiblechanging points of view in the same formulation or expression
Conflict	3. Value-Assumption: Departmental equality versus Infallibility Artifact-effect: Difference in speaking time creates doubt about whether infallibility applies to everyone	4. Value-Assumption: Equality of tasks versus The family works Artifact-effect: Hierarchical technology demonstrates organizational differences

Integrating Effects of Artifacts

The division into sectional territories is a prominent artifact both in relation to physical manifestations and technology. Inside the department, sectional territories have an important integrating effect, helping to reduce the tensions between the assumptions that 'this belongs to us' and the value of 'cross-organizational collaboration'. The members' own self-understanding presents interorganizational collaboration as desirable, but the location of the various sections and the technological dependence of each section as operations technology makes it impossible to work together and, thus, provides the organizational members with explanations and justifications why collaboration is not possible. The artifact level here integrates assumptions of 'ownership' and the stated value of collaboration using considerations of practicality and rationality based on the artifact level. Instead of having severe conflicts threatening the internal integration of the organizational culture, the artifact level makes it possible for the members of the organization to behave according to the basic assumptions and still keep up the intentions of collaboration.

The indirect speech also has an integrating effect on the consistent relation between the value of 'serving the minister' and the basic assumption of 'passive adaptation', which further emphasizes the cultural importance of the minister to the organization. Indirect speech permits the members of the organization to alter their views while retaining the same formulation. This helps them maintain a flexible adaptation which prevents conflict with the minister no matter what the minister wants. The indirect speech also makes it possible for the organizational members to experience a stable and continuous minister service, while at the same time adapting to the discontinuity and instability of political life.

The Conflict-creating Effect of Artifacts

Conversely, the hierarchical organization technology creates conflicts between the ideas of 'task equality' and 'familyness'. Artifacts centered on power and status are predictable within the department and therefore they do not imply an active conflict-creating effect disturbing the 'family peace', but in the long-term it becomes difficult for the members to maintain the familyness within a still more explicit organizational hierarchy.

Finally, differences in speaking time between organization members with different status generate tensions between the assumptions of 'departmental equality' and 'infallibility'. The tensions are based on the assumption that the individual department heads cannot learn from others. However, differences in speaking time indicate that some heads of sections have more to say than others. Acknowledgement of such differences would cast doubt on whether all sections possess equal amounts of 'infallibility'. Such equality is essential to preserve the internal balance.

The Effects of Artifacts

Based on these small examples, the artifact level can be analyzed in terms of its effect on values and basic assumptions. From the analysis of the relationships between particular values and basic assumptions, the artifact level may be deciphered in the sense that it becomes possible to distinguish between the artifacts having a stable and distinct effect within the culture (whether it is integrating or conflict-creating) and the artifacts, reflecting actual fashions and conjunctural circumstances within the organization.

The analysis only shows small examples, but it is important to emphasize that the same artifacts may have several effects in relation to the culture's many relations between values and basic assumptions. Indirect speech, for example, supports the relation between passive adaptation to the minister, but also works as an integrating secret code in relation to the tensions between the value of shared attitude and the assumption that 'we are at the center of things'. Ethnocentrism obtains a contents via a common secret code which nobody else can interpret, and which the environment therefore views as an expression of a shared attitude inside the departement.

In the context of the examples of the artifact level's effects in relation to values and basic assumptions, we can formulate two assertions which can be expanded in the execution of a more comprehensive cultural analysis:

1. The artifact level may have an integrating and/or conflict-creating effect in relation to values and basic assumptions.
2. The same artifact may have different effects in terms of its relation to values and basic assumptions.

Consequences for the Functionalist Funnel Model

If retracing our steps from basic assumptions to values and artifacts is valid, we must conclude that Schein's model of a hierarchical distribution into three analytical levels may be further elaborated. There are several reasons for this.

First, the relations between values and basic assumptions are not exclusively characterized by consistency but also contain inconsistency and unclarity, where value and assumption do not fit together. In the study of the department, inconsistency between values and assumptions is a distinct characteristic of the organizational culture. This can create considerable tensions and problems within the organization, but the existence of tensions between cognitive levels does not automatically mean that the culture's survival is threatened, nor does it mean that the culture is about to collapse.

Second, in contrast to Schein, who applies the artifact level as a pathway to the cultural analysis, the artifact level used here has a much more autonomous effect in relation to values and basic assumptions. This effect may be either integrating or conflict-creating. The values and basic assumptions are both cognitive elements to which relations can be constructed. The artifact level, in contrast, has no autonomous cognitive contents. Its contents depends on the effect of the artifact within the overall organizational culture.

The integrating effect derives from the artifact level's role as the local rationality which is adapted to values and/or basic assumptions. Compared with values and assumptions, it is easier for members of an organization to manipulate artifacts in a desired direction. Several artifacts such as linguistic expressions and stories are especially sensitive to change in the organization's conditions for external adaptation and internal integration. The artifact level can also have a conflict-creating effect. Various types of artifacts may create conflicts from tradition-based ways of talking to the physical space of the organization. Also, the scope of this conflict-creating effect may vary inside the organization from threatening key assumptions of the cultural paradigm to cause minor disturbances in the relationship between values and basic assumptions.

The data material here is too narrow to make any general conclusions in relation to Schein's analytical model, but our experiences so far can provide a foundation for the following analysis of the cultural diagnosis.

The Diagnosis of Organizational Culture

The functionalist diagnosis of organizational culture moves, as does Schein's basic model, up and down through different analytical levels. The analysis is first narrowed down to include the cultural paradigm, which establishes the deeper, stable foundation of the organizational culture. We then bring the cultural paradigm in relation to the two superordinate levels: values and artifacts. Values express a more situation-dependent search for new solutions to organizational problems, whereas the artifact level holds the culture 'in check' in its daily execution of tasks.

The cultural diagnosis can therefore be carried out on the basis of several different phases in the cultural analysis, where the choice of cultural diagnosis depends on why the organizational culture is being analyzed. In a comparison of several different organizational cultures where the goal is to elaborate basic similarities and differences, the cultural paradigm is in focus because values and artifacts seen in a comparative light are expressions of conjunctural or short-lived 'pendulum swings' in the culture. Regardless of changing tasks and fashionable artifacts, the cultural paradigm constitutes the foundation for understanding the apparent confusion and changeability of the cultural surface phenomena.

However, if the purpose of the analysis is to try and consciously change the organization, the relations between the three cultural levels becomes the central factor. Identifying tensions between levels can help to reveal those areas in the culture which can form the starting point for 'unfreezing' the organizational culture. The culture's strong, consistent relations, however, give an indication of those areas in which there might arise resistance to change. An apparently marginal change of artifacts could penetrate deeply through the 'support pillars' which hold together the values and basic assumptions. Hence, all levels in the functionalist cultural analysis must be part of the evaluation of how a cultural diagnosis can be utilized in attempts at consciously planned organizational change.

Compared to the symbolic cultural perspective which follows, the functionalist perspective has been depicted only from a single organization in a ministry, the department. The justification for this is that functionalist procedure would be the same regardless of what organization is analyzed. An analysis of the culture of a lower ranking directorate, while it would yield additional results, would add no new analytical dimensions to the funnel model. The contents of the functionalist cultural analysis, however, varies according to which functions have the most important significance for the organization's survival.

Chapter 4
A Symbolic Perspective

In contrast to the functionalist perspective, the symbolic perspective in the study of organizations originates from a wide range of theoretical traditions. Concepts and ideas from anthropology, semiotics, literary criticism, communication studies all contribute to the 'melting pot', which has been labelled organizational symbolism. At the outset, symbolism can be viewed as a reaction to the functionalist perspective, and it tends to be 'defined by and exists in conceptual bondage with the functionalist paradigm' (Putnam, 1983:8). However, in recent years, organizational symbolism has developed a still more elaborate framework for studying organizations as cultures (Putnam, 1983; Turner, 1990; Gagliardi, 1992; Alvesson and Berg, 1992).

Symbolism as discussed here draws primarily upon the study of symbols in an organizational context, but it is also inspired by semiotics (the latter being the study of the meaning of signs) (Pondy et al., 1983; Frost et al., 1985: Smircich, 1983a; Broms and Gahmberg, 1987; Sapienza, 1985; Barley, 1983). In this book, we will also follow a widely used anthropological approach to symbol theory (Geertz, 1973; 1983) as well as ideas drawn from text analysis.

Symbolism

Symbolism is a diffuse label which stretches from an interpretation-oriented *verstehen* perspective (Putnam and Pacanowsky, 1983) to a view of symbol creation as an expression of that which is uniquely human:

> Hence, instead of defining man as an animal *rationale*, we should define him as an animal *symbolicum*. By doing so we can highlight the difference between humans and animals, and we can understand the new way open to man – the way to civilization (Cassirer, 1944:26).

The Creation of Meaning

The point of departure within symbolism is that individuals seek and create meaning for themselves and their environment. The symbolic paradigm assumes that humans actively define and create their own reality. Reality is not objects to which people simply react. Rather, reality is social constructions within which people act using their own definition of the situation. These social constructions derive from a collective creation of meaning whereby the same actions can be accorded different meanings.

Because people are considered to be active creators of their own reality, it is important to understand the processes by which meanings are created and linked to individual actions. 'Social reality is not a static series of social facts' (Ritzer, 1975:96), but the result of a creative process whereby 'people interpret or define each other's actions instead of simply reacting to them' (Ritzer, 1975:96). Thus, the interpretative processes shared by members of organizations provide the conditions necessary in order to develop shared definitions of the organizational reality.

In contrast to the organic metaphor within organizational theory which regards organizations as organisms struggling for survival (Scott, 1992; Morgan, 1986), the symbolic perspective regards organizations as human systems. In the symbolic perspective, actions do not take place according to a mechanical cause-effect relationship nor out of functional suitability, but according to the kind of meaning different actions have for the organization's members. The organizational reality thus becomes a symbolic universe in which organizational members act according to the defined meaning of things and actions in the organization (Cassirer, 1944): 'The central message of symbolism is that humans act (symbolically), organisms behave' (Pondy, 1983:22).

Symbols: The Expression of Meaning

A thing, an action, etc. becomes a symbol when it represents something more than itself. Things and actions become symbols when they are not viewed in their instrumental sense, but are instead experienced according to the meaning conferred on them by the organization's members; for example when the large desk is viewed not as an instrumental need for a lot of paperwork, but as an expression of power, status and influence. Hence:

> A symbol is a sign which denotes something much greater than itself, and which calls for the association of certain conscious or unconscious ideas, in order for it to be endowed with its full meaning and significance (Pondy, 1983:5).

Thus, when creating symbols members of organizations invest meaning in them. They construct the meaning of things and actions as an ongoing process in organizations, where old symbols loose their evocative character as expressions of meaning and new symbols are created as significant expressions of how organizational members make sense of their organizational life (Cohen, 1985; Gioia and Pitre, 1990).

Some of the symbolic expressions that occur in organizations are constructed consciously and deliberately in order to create a desired effect, like the simple symbols of power in a senior executive office: 'The size, layout and decor often shout out symbolically "I am the boss". The office is designed to impress upon all who enter that a person of importance works here' (Pondy, 1983:8). Other symbolic expressions may be more subtle and tell much about the every day interpretations among the members of the organization. For instance, the small name tags on the managers' doors are turned into symbols by the organizational members of a distant and repressed relationship between managers and employees.

Symbols in a Semiotic Context

Within semiotics and text analysis things/actions and meaning are referred to, respectively, as signifier, the material object, and the signified, which is its meaning. In the example of the senior office the large desk is the 'signifier' or the expression and the associated power its 'signified' contents. However, they are only divided for analytical purposes: in practice a symbol is always a 'thing-plus-meaning' (Barthes, 1990)*. This is exemplified by Barthes with his discussion of a bouquet of roses.

> Take a bunch of roses: I use it to *signify* my passion. Do we have here, then, only a signifier and a signified, the roses and my passion? Not even that: to put it accurately, there are here only "passionified" roses. But on the plane of analysis, we do have three terms; for these roses weighted with passion perfectly and correctly allow themselves to be decomposed into roses and passion: the former and the latter existed before uniting and forming this third object, which is the sign (Barthes, 1990:113).

Here, the roses represent something else and something far more than themselves: warm feelings. However, in other situations they may repre-

---

* Within semiotics the unification of signifier and signified is labelled a sign, which signifies a relationship between these elements. In contrast the important characteristic of symbols is that 'all symbols are created subjectively and are invested with a particular kind of subjective meaning' (Pondy, 1983:5). Here, I don't distinguish between signs and symbols, but prefer to build on the more common sense understanding of symbols within organization theory.

sent a nostalgic goodbye or a warning of danger. The more complex the entities, events and actions are, the more possibilities for alternative creations of meaning. The associations which create symbols may derive from any source: a phenomenon's similarity to other phenomena, peoples' experiences, knowledge of conventions and dreams about the future. Thus, by studying symbols, a window is opened to the study of interpretative, emotional and aesthetic aspects of organizational life.

The Multidimensional Reality

Despite the differences between functionalism and symbolism they are both products of systems thinking in the sense that they both view culture as a social, integrated pattern. 'Cultural systems must have a minimum degree of coherence, else we would not call them systems; and by observation, they normally have a great deal more' (Geertz, 1973:17-18). However, from a cultural perspective cultural systems are more than is suggested by functionalism, they are subjective and they are carriers of multiple interpretations.

Culture as System

Organizational culture as a system does not refer to distinct features of reality. Rather, it is a specific way of viewing the organizational reality (abstractions) that is different from the ways in which formal and informal social structures view organizations (Scott, 1992). The organizational culture contains its own logic and its own set of concepts, which focus primarily on the interpretative processes and the creation of meaning in everyday life. In contrast the formal and informal social structures focus on the issues of goal-specification and formalization (formal structures) and patterns of human interrelation developed in order to provide organizational survival (informal structure) (Scott, 1992).

This simultaneous organizational existence of the abstractions of cultural system and social structure is expressed by Geertz:

> Culture is the fabric of meaning in terms of which human beings interpret their experience and guide their action; social structure is the form that action takes, the actually existing network of social relations. Culture and social structure are then but abstractions from the same phenomena. The one considers social action in respect to its meaning for those who carry it out, the other considers it in terms of its contribution to the functioning of some social system (Geertz, 1973:145).

In the relationship between organizational culture and social system the symbolic perspective distinguishes itself from functionalism in several ways.

First, within functionalism organizational culture is integrated into the total social system wherein culture fulfills a supplementary function in the internal integration and external adaptation necessary to organizational survival. Symbolism, in contrast, defines culture as an independent system linked with, but different from, the social system. Culture is not necessarily integrated into the social system, but contains its own independent definition of reality. Culture can therefore come into conflict with the social system; e.g. the organizational culture may contain an independent socially defined hierarchy which may differ radically from the hierarchy defined by the formal structure.

Second, functionalism assumes that systems are in balance and thus emphasizes culture's integrative and harmony-creating function. In contrast, symbolism does not automatically assume any predetermined relations within the culture nor between culture and the social system. The symbolic perspective provides the possibility for local creation of meaning within different organizational units and contexts within the organization, and hence, the existence of different, inconsistent patterns of meaning within organizational culture.

A Multiplicity of Interpretations

Symbolism thus assumes that reality is subjective and multidimensional. The same organizational reality provides several possible interpretations, which together create the socially defined reality. This is not to say that a stone is not a stone within symbolism. The determinant factor is what kind of meaning the stone is accorded by the organization's members. The multidimensional reality of symbolism expresses itself in two different ways.

On the one hand, different kinds of meaning may be associated with the same phenomenon within the organization. In metaphorical terms, the stone can be viewed by members of the organization as a burdensome millstone, as a beautiful sculpture or as an expression of solidity and strength. Here, different groups of people interpret and define the same phenomenon each in their own way within the organization. Multiple meanings converge in one phenomenon, creating a rather vague expression of meanings; for instance the existence of different interpretations within an organization of a weekly meeting like the heart of power, the old timers parade and the dog and pony show create a vague symbolic expression of the meeting.

On the other hand, the same meaning can be expressed in different phenomena; for example, in the science fiction film 'Close Encounters of the Third Kind', where the innocent earthling is obsessed with the image of a mountain, which he molds first from clay, but then from his mashed potatoes and shaving cream! Here, several very different objects express the same meaning, creating rather strong symbolic expressions. This relationship between meaning and phenomena is conscious in the formation of corporate identity programs (Olins, 1989), where design, architecture, layout and graphics are deliberately used to express the same notion of identity.

With its multidimensional view of reality, symbolism destroys our image of a single all-encompassing truth in organizations, helping us instead to discover the existence of many small truths within the same organization. From a symbolic perspective, organizational culture can therefore never be elucidated completely. Understanding an organization's culture is, rather, a continuing and systematized creative process which attempts to reconstruct the organization members' processes of creating meaning (Berger and Luckmann, 1966; Ritzer, 1975).

This multiplicity expressed by symbols has been formulated in a more elaborated definition of symbols, than the one used beforehand. Here, symbols are 'objects, acts, relationships or linguistic formations that stand ambiguously for a multiplicity of meanings, evoke emotions and impel men to action' (Cohen, 1976:23). Following this direction, organizational culture cannot be extracted from the bottom of the organizational depths as a consistent pattern of meaning, but must be discovered and elaborated via many series of interpretations. The interpretations are not different vertical levels of analysis, but interrelated associated images: 'What we call our data are really our own constructions of other peoples' constructions of what they and their compatriots are up to' (Geertz, 1973:9), or to put it another way: culture upon culture upon culture.

Webs of Meaning

The definitions of culture used by most symbolic analysts tend to be quite general:

> That man is an animal suspended in webs of significance he himself has spun, I take culture to be those webs, and the analysis of it to be therefore not an experimental science in search of law but an interpretative one in search of meaning (Geertz, 1973:5).

Culture as webs of meaning, organized in terms of symbols and representations... to study social significance – how things, events and interactions come to be meaningful (Smircich, 1985:63).

Sum total of ways of living, organizing and communing built up in a group of human being and transmitted to newcomers by means of verbal and nonverbal communication (Bormann, 1983:199).

The structural dimension of a corporate culture can be seen as a symbolic field. This field is essentially a holographic pattern of clustered symbolic representations which constitute reality in organization (Berg, 1985:285).

The definitions by Geertz (1973) and Smircich (1985) both use the image of 'web' in order to describe the interrelated patterns of meanings which result from the numerous interpretations developed among human beings. Thus, the study of organizational culture becomes not only the study of the ways in which members of organizations turn things, events and interactions into meaningful symbols; it also searches for relations between the various symbols in order to discover the 'webs of meanings' between them. The existence of relations between different symbols is also stressed by Berg (1985) in the notion of clustered symbolic representations. Finally, Bormann (1983) stresses the importance of the communication processes, which create and maintain the shared symbolic reality and transmit the 'webs of meaning' from one organizational generation to the next.

As the most general concept describing organizational culture I believe that 'ways of living' (Bormann, 1983) encapsulates organizational culture's special focus because it indicates both that people live differently, and that these differences tend to fall into social patterns. Taking Geertz' general definition, and the concepts elaborated by Bormann and Berg, organizational culture is here defined as follows:

Organizational culture consists of the organization members' socially defined and meaningful realities, which reflect the organization's special way of life. These meaningful realities can be perceived as patterns of interrelated symbolic expressions, which evolve and are maintained especially via myths, organizational stories and rituals.

Thus, organizational culture is seen as patterns or webs of various kinds of symbolic expressions indicating that these expressions (e.g. various power symbols) are linked together by the members of the organization, forming meaningful relationships. The study of organizational culture, then, searches for the relationships between symbolic forms and expressions in order to construct the pattern or web between them. This cultural definition builds on the presumed existence of various key symbolic expressions (Ortner, 1973), e.g. physical symbols, behavioral symbols like rituals, and verbal symbols like stories and myths. However, the symbolic perspective does not presuppose a distinct relationship between those key symbolic expressions, e.g. symbols, myths and stories, but expects them to be interrelated in various ways according to the particular organizational culture.

Thus, in contrast to the predefined relations between artifacts, values and basic assumptions within the functionalist perspective, symbolism consists of many key symbolic expressions which can be interrelated in many different combinations. This is not to say that all of the key symbolic expressions are necessary in order to obtain insights into a particular organizational culture. Rather they constitute a systematization of possible steps toward gaining insight into the organizational culture.

Symbols

Individual symbols have been described in terms of their degree of visibility, the level of consciousness in their formation and their function for the organization (Dandridge, 1983; Pondy, 1983; Daft, 1983; Berg, 1985; Alvesson and Berg, 1992). These sets of definitions and classifications have a common point of departure. They all view symbols as deriving from various basic elements (signs) which are then ascribed meaning. The signs may take the form of any of the following:

1. an object;
2. an action;
3. an event;
4. an utterance;
5. a picture.

Symbols can thus be seen, heard, felt or in other ways perceived by human beings. The individual symbol combines different signs and associations into a meaningful whole. Members of an organization do not necessarily experience the same symbols. The symbolic perspective does not presume any consensus among the organization's members in their understanding of organizational phenomena. The individual symbol is therefore not necessarily assumed to be part of a larger whole within the culture.

The symbolic perspective distinguishes between different types of symbols:

1. *Physical symbols* or artifacts are defined as physical objects, which are assigned meaning by organizational members. The organization's architecture and physical layout, the members' physical placement, attire, the graphic design of internal memos and internal correspondence, the design of the corporate identity (logos, stickers, markers etc.) of the organization are examples of physical entities which can be used as expressions of meaning.

2. *Behavioral symbols* comprise those acts in the organization which are ascribed a meaning beyond their instrumental contents. Rituals and ceremonies are examples of strongly symbolic behavioral acts.
3. *Verbal symbols*, not to be confused with language itself, are those linguistic forms with a symbolic contents. Myths, stories, metaphors, special phrases, jokes, slogans and jargon are examples of verbal symbols in organizations.

The symbolic perspective raises the question of whether the individual symbols are distinct, local symbols in the organization created depending on time and place, or whether they are part of a larger cohesive pattern of interpretations which penetrates and holds the organization together. These patterns between symbols are here elaborated using the concepts of world view and ethos.

The following analysis of the culture of a concrete organization focuses on some selected behavioral and verbal symbols: namely, rituals, myths, sagas and stories.

Physical Symbols: Objects

In recent literature on organizational symbolism, physical symbols have received an increasing attention, most signifiantly in the contributions in Gagliardi (1992).

At the outset, the physical symbols have been very important in the study of the visible expressions of the organizational culture, as they are often condensed expressions of the much more subtle patterns of meaning. The distinct power symbols in the organization may serve as pathways in order to grasp the meaning of power to its members. This notion of using physical symbols as a way to reach an understanding of the cultural pattern of meaning has been labelled 'the hermeneutic dimension' by Gagliardi (1992:21). Gagliardi argues that physical symbols opposed to other types of symbolic expressions like rituals are very sensitive to shifts in the organizational culture, as the physical setting is such a fundamental aspect of everyday life in organizational life that it is permanently being reconstructed and reinterpreted:

> We can, in fact, "rehearse" for the time a ritual that no longer has meaning for us, we can send out false messages about our identity, we can give an artifactual image about our identity, but we can't live for too long in an artifactual setting inconsistent with... our culture (Gagliardi, 1992:25).

A wide selection of physical symbols have been studied along the hermeneutic dimension, relating the symbols to patterns of meaning. For example, Berg and Kreiner (1992) show how corporate architecture may serve as symbols of strategic profile and status, as physical symbols are here constructed deliberately by the organization in order to influence the organizational culture. On the other hand, Larsen and Schultz (1992) show how the emergent setting of physical symbols within an organization may serve as an unintended pathway to grasp the root-metaphor (here: a monastery) which highlights the culture of the organization.

Apart from serving as expressions of the underlying patterns of meaning, Gagliardi claims that physical symbols are claimed to influence the organizational culture in their own right. Instead of focusing on the role of physical symbols in organizational sense-making, physical symbols also influence the 'senses' of the organizational members. Thus, physical symbols delimit and structure the sensory experience of organizational members, especially in relation to time and space.

> The selective stimuli – visual, aural, olfactory, tactile -transmitted by the habitat created by the organization accustom us... to use our senses in a different way, so that the same event can be perceived in one setting entirely differently from the way it is perceived in another (Gagliardi, 1992:18).

Thus, a cultural event like a meeting may be experienced and interpreted differently by the organizational members, if it takes place in the old, dark and decorated meeting room with a large, polished table or if it takes place in the new atrium building with soft, white furniture and lots of light. The opportunities for interaction as well as the ways the physical setting are intuitively sensed both originate from the physical symbols in their own right. This way of perceiving physical symbols has been labelled the pragmatic dimension (Gagliardi, 1992).

In both the study of the hermeneutic and pragmatic dimension of physical symbols, the focus is to obtain an understanding of how physical symbols express and influence the organizational culture as it is created and recreated among the organizational members.

Furthermore, physical symbols have been used as more deliberate tools for identity formation and image-building (Olins, 1989). The use of physical symbols as markers of the corporate identity is an expanding field within management and includes a wide range of identity component from product design to architecture, and graphic design of communication material to the use of logos and brands as means of internal and external communication. Here, the physical symbols are analyzed and manipulated in relation to their ability to create and express the corporate identity of the organization, which by Olins is defined as:

> Products/services: What you make or sell.
> Environments: Where you make or sell it – the place or physical context.
> Information: How you describe and publicize what you do.

Behavior: How people within the organization behave to each other and to outsiders (Olins, 1989:29).

Thus, the study of physical symbols in itself contains a number of opportunities both for obtaining knowledge about the organizational culture and for the development of corporate identity.

Behavioral Symbols: Rituals

Rituals are symbolic acts carried out systematically and linked to specific situations. Only a few rituals are dictated by the formal structure, instead they tend to be tradition-bound rules for how one ought to behave in certain situations. They act as guidelines for interpreting and evaluating the actions of others. Rituals have been defined as:

a rule-governed activity of a symbolic character which draws the attention of its participants to objects of thought and feeling which they hold to be of special significance (as cited in Kunda, 1991:87).
They involve (1) relatively elaborate and planned sets of activities, (2) carried out through social interaction, (3) usually for the benefit of an audience, (4) with multiple social consequences (Trice and Beyer, 1984:655).

In other words, rituals are 'social dramas with well-defined roles for people to perform' (Trice and Beyer, 1984:655). Among the rituals in daily organizational life greeting-rituals and rituals of how and where to take your lunch are well-known in studies of organizational culture. Also, meeting-rituals (Schultz, 1991) may serve as a significant point of departure for understanding how the members of an organization are expected to behave in meeting-situations, and how they interpret these events in the organization.

Typically, a meeting-ritual has evolved from a specific purpose, like monthly planning among managers, and the participants may have interpreted the meetings as an important contribution in the long-term planning of the organization – and perhaps they still do. However, the meaning of the ritual may also change, e.g. by turning into a monthly demarkation of each manager's turf. Even though the contents of a ritual's meaning may change over time, a ritual may retain its original form. A ritual may appear unchanged but generate numerous varied meanings for members of the organization.

Analyzing rituals within organizational culture involves several questions:

1. Determining what kind of social situation the ritual addresses in the organization (lunch, meetings, greetings, etc.).

2. Determining the location of the ritual in time and space in the organization (e.g. special sacred places).
3. Describing what kind of behavior and expressions the ritual forbids and prescribes to the participants (e.g. prescription of chief and indians, gestures and articulation, etc.).
4. Determining the meaning ascribed to the ritual by the organization's members.

Rituals form standardized behavioral patterns in the organization and can be found in a wide range of everyday situations. The ritual repertoire of an organization might include a number of different types of rituals, each prescribing and forbidding the behavior in a distinct situation and having different social consequences.

Trice and Beyer (1984) discuss different types of rituals and their manifest, expressive social consequences, each of which plays an important role in the organization. These include:

1. Rituals of transition: induction and basic training.
2. Rituals of degradation: firing and replacing.
3. Rituals of celebration: seminars and staged events.
4. Rituals of rebirth: organizational development activities.
5. Rituals for conflict reduction: collective bargaining.
6. Rituals of integration: office parties, Christmas party.

Furthermore, Kunda (1991) shows how rituals are used in the managerial attempts to orchestrate the organizational culture in a number of different training and teaching situations. Here, the use of rituals are clear examples of attempts to conduct normative control in relation to the members of the organization, and Kunda provides detailed examples of how organizational members react to these very elaborated and evocative rituals by role-embracement and role-distancing.

It is not my intention here to classify or describe the gamut of organizational rituals. Rather, our goal will be to identify those which express important features of the organizational culture.

Verbal Symbols: Myths, Sagas and Stories

Studies of organizational culture address a variety of verbal symbols and other kinds of verbal expressions of cultural significance (Filby and Wilmott, 1988; Clark, 1977; Martin et al., 1983; Pondy, 1983; Wilkins, 1983; Broms and Gahmberg, 1983; 1987). Myths, sagas, and stories are among the most significant verbal symbolic expressions and will be dealt with here. However, platitudes and labels (Czarniawska-Joerges, 1988), jokes

(Hatch and Ehrlich, 1993), pet-names and slang may also be significant cultural expressions.

Myths

Among the most important studies of myths are those of Barthes (1990) and Westerlund and Sjøstrand (1979) and Levi-Strauss (1968). The organizational culture literature also contains several contributions to the understanding of myths in culture (Christensen and Molin, 1983; Molin, 1987; Abravanel, 1983; Broms and Gahmberg, 1983; Filby and Wilmott, 1988; Pondy, 1983).

Following Christensen and Molin myths can be defined as

> a shared unreflected everyday explanation which serves as the norm of decision-making, and thereby legitimates choices of action and reproduces the dominant cultural patterns (Christensen and Molin, 1983:55).

A myth is thus a standardized explanation with roots in the organization's history. Myths evolve in order to structure and explain experiences in a meaningful and clear way.

> Myth does not deny things... it organizes a world which is without contradiction because it is without depth, a world wide open and wallowing in the evident, it establishes blissful clarity (Barthes, 1990:143).

Beyond this, myth often has a fundamental legendary character with a strong impact which distinguishes the myth from the myriad of minor explanations of everyday life. Myth does not derive from actual organizational reality, but from a transference of historical events to actual reality. The mythological everyday explanation can take on different forms, including:

1. A repeated application of once successful solutions to other situations without regard to whether the solution is appropriate;
2. explanations of the organization's 'present state' which intermittently affect the organization;
3. explanations of what the future will bring and what kinds of demands the future is making on the present, based on historical experience.

Myths have a dual function within organizations (Molin, 1987); first, they legitimate the members' choice of action. Myths are central to understanding how organizational culture structures individual and social acts. Second, myth helps the organizational culture to maintain its world view. Myth revitalizes the organization's world view via a myriad of concrete everyday explanations in specific situations. The organizational culture's world view becomes visible at the moment the myth is told and transferred from the organization's 'elders' to the new members. At the same time, myth constitutes a source for the evolution and change in the world view of the organization's members. New events and persons give rise to the formulation of new myths which may initially create differences in perceptions of reality, but which eventually enter into the members' shared world view.

Sagas and Stories

The unique explanatory character of myths distinguishes it from the organizational saga, which Bormann and Berg define as

> the shared fantasies, the rhetorical visions and the narratives of achievements, events, goals and ideal states of the entire organization (Bormann, 1983:115).
>
> The saga of an organization, with its heroes, scapegoats, battles and victories, and the likes gives members symbolically loaded points of reference, organized in time (Berg, 1985:286).
>
> An organizational saga is a collective understanding of unique accomplishment in a formally established group. The group's definition of the accomplishment, intrinsically historical but embellished through retelling and rewriting, links stages of organizational development (Clark, 1977:178).

Organizational sagas are thus shared narratives which contribute to the creation and evolution of a shared identity for the organization. In contrast to myths, sagas are linked to the organization's actual history and are important in the transmission of historical accomplishments. Sagas have a unique, dramatic, and historically 'real' character, which rises above the concrete time and place and serves as a reminder of organizational history. Sagas may evoke emotions such as laughter, indignation and curiosity.

In this respect sagas are similar to organizational stories, which refer to shared anecdotes describing a single event sequence:

> An organizational story focuses on a single, unified sequence of events, apparently drawn from the institution's history. The heroes and heroines of such stories are organizational members (Martin et al., 1983:439).

Compared to sagas, stories are less pretentious in the description of past accomplishments and the linking of organizational development. Stories may, indeed, also refer to day to day events that highlight general themes and evoke emotions. However, sagas and stories do have several important characteristics in common:

1. Refer to actual events in the organization's history;
2. highlight a general theme or commentary on the current situation and thus distinguish themselves from small talk or gossip (as characterized by Deal and Kennedy, 1982:87-98);
3. contain a dramatic form or contents which evokes fantasy, emotion and a sense of drama.

Patterns between Symbols

The members of the organization may create shared patterns of meaning or interpretative codes (Barley, 1983) that link the organization's various symbols and that must be interpreted by the person seeking to understand the organizational culture (hereafter called the interpreter) in order for the culture to be adequately understood.

World View and Ethos

In the description of cultural patterns one can distinguish between the cognitive world view that contains the organization members' mental image of reality, and the ethos, which comprises the members' aesthetic and moral view of themselves and of life in general.

Clifford Geertz defines these concepts as a group's (or in my terms an organization's):

1. *World view:* 'picture of the way things actually are, their concept of nature, of self, of society. It contains their most comprehensive ideas of order' (Geertz, 1973:127);
2. *ethos:* 'the tone, character and quality of life, its moral and aesthetic style and mood... [as] the underlying attitude towards themselves and their world that life reflects' (Geertz, 1973:127).

Whereas Schein sees values and basic assumptions as being deduced from each other, this is not true of world view or ethos. Neither provides a more correct picture of the organinational culture. Rather, they create different images of the organizational culture's contents. Ethos and world view enter into a more reciprocal relationship:

> The ethos is made intellectually reasonable by being shown to represent a way of life implied by the actual state of affairs which the world view describes, and the world view is made emotionally acceptable by being presented as an image of an actual state of affairs of which such a way of life is an authentic expression (Geertz, 1973:127).

Both world view and ethos are comprehensive, often ambiguous concepts that represent the member's shared or varied images of the culture. Hence, one cannot set forth different methods for deciphering a world view or an ethos. Here, we can profitably employ text analysis, which is well suited for analyzing collective structures of meaning based on studies of the language of the organizational members.

Metaphors and Metonyms

Metaphors and metonyms are useful concepts for revealing general cultural images because they aggregate the creation of meanings in organizations (Raspa, 1992; Larsen and Schultz, 1992; Sapienza, 1985; Berg, 1985; Barley, 1983; Broms and Gahmberg, 1987; Morgan, 1986; Brown, 1977). Metaphors and metonyms are images expressed through the language in the organization whether it is spoken or written. They may appear in close relation to the verbal symbols of the organizational culture, e.g. a 'garage' metaphor describes the good old days in the organizational myth of the founding of the organization; but metaphors and metonyms may also appear as general expressions of their own.

Metaphors are meanings derived via similarity or analogy. They depict certain entities and events as if they were other entities and events. When a governmental administration is described as if it were a monastery, or when the civil servant 'plows through heaps of cases', the metaphor may reveal new aspects of the organizational culture and emphasize the organization's symbolic aspects. An organizational culture described as a monastery, a modern total institution or an anthill thus inspire quite different associations.

Some metaphors in organization are chosen carefully and deliberately by the management in order to create shared associations among the members of the organization, like when the top management of Scandinavian Airlines used the metaphor of 'building a cathedral' in the launching of the strategy in the 1980s of the 'Businessman's Airline'. However, the symbolic perspective will first of all look for the metaphors expressing the patterns of meaning created by the members of the organization in everyday life. This way of using metaphors has been labelled 'root-metaphor', as it sees the metaphorical image as the heart of the organizational culture:

> at the heart of tacit of informal knowledge what are to be found are concrete images rather than philosophies (Gagliardi, 1992:27).

In contrast to metaphor, a metonym is an aspect or a thing which stands for the whole, such as the crown for the power of the king, or the quill pen for an old-style bureaucrat.

Metaphors and metonyms enter into the understanding of an organizational culture. The metaphors used by the organization's members provide a pathway to cultural understanding. In looking for metaphors ask specific questions when studying the organization: for example, What are the central metaphors in the organization? How are they developed in relation to the environments, neighbouring cultures, self-understanding? What kinds of metonyms link everyday life in connection with the moral aesthetic conceptions in the organization?

Furthermore, metaphors and metonyms are used to interpret and formulate visual representations of the organizational culture. If the organization is envisioned as a 'monastery' the interpreter may start to ask what the monastery looks like, where the monks are located in the organization, when and how do the monks communicate with God, etc. The metaphor may reveal the members' mental picture of their organization and encourage the interpreter to provide a visual presentation of the organizational culture. Thus, metaphors are simple, effective ways to communicate the principal contents of a comprehensive cultural interpretation.

The Actant Model

In addition to looking for metaphors and metonyms, the interpreter may look for narrative patterns in the world view and ethos as defined among the members of the organization. Here, a narrative pattern is defined as the story-line in the members' interpretation of organizational reality. Opposed to the story as a concrete and explicitly expressed verbal symbol, the story-line of the narrative pattern describes the members' often tacit interpretations of how things, events and persons are linked together. Thus, the goal is to discover the system or pattern which is embedded in the language of the organizational members, when they talk and express themselves in actions.

The 'actant model', is one of several models from text analysis which is used here to describe narrative patterns of culture (Berthelsen, 1974; Brandt-Pedersen and Rønn-Poulsen, 1980). The actant-model analysis attempts to map out the patterns, rules or developmental sequences typical of the narrative of the respective genre. Such genres may range from the fairy tale's ugly duckling, which is transformed into a white swan and is rewarded with the princess and half the kingdom, to the spy novel's initial confusion which evolves into knowledge and its moral as a game without winners. The question here is whether the organizational culture's world view and ethos also contain a narrative pattern which provides insight into the contents of the two key concepts.

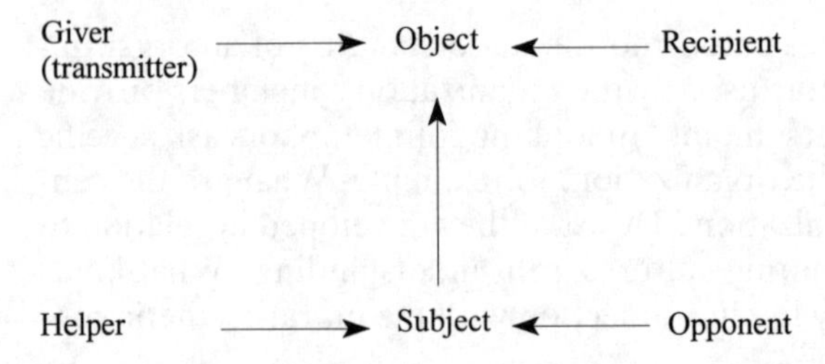

Figure 4.1. The Actant Model (from Brandt-Petersen and Rønn-Poulson, 1980:47)

The model used here is Greimas' formulation of the 'actant model', which can best be described as an ideal-typical role list for narratives. The model describes a relational pattern between six different actants which make up a typical sequence of action in a narrative. One actant is the subject, who (or which) has will, knowledge and ability to act (the prince). It is assumed that the subject is in pursuit of an object (the princess), which the subject desires in order to give it to a recipient (the prince himself). Here there appears a giver, who has the object but would like to relinquish/transmit it onward (the old king). In the course of the narrative there may appear both helpers and opponents; the helpers can be the old witch and the opponents the black dragons. The actant model is illustrated in Figure 4.1.

The model is based on two assumptions: First, the actant is *not* an actor. Actants are not necessarily persons, and the same person or phenomenon can in the course of a story, change from being an opponent, for example, to a helper, or have the role of both subject and recipient. Rather, actants are 'positions in the narrative game'. Second, not all actants are necessarily actively involved in the sequence of the narrative. Rather, they help to focus our attention on the key elements of the narrative. For example, a narrative pattern does not always have to contain recipients or helpers.

The model's utility in understanding the world view and ethos is not that it clarifies the actions as they in fact take place. Rather, the actant model is a method of systematizing how the narrative sequences are experienced and constructed within the organizational culture: who is the subject? What/whom is being sought? What is viewed as obstacle (opponents) and as potential forces (helpers) in the organization? Is there anyone or anything that always has the role of giver? Who are the recipients? The subject himself, others within the organization, abstract notions of groups in the society, etc.?

The analysis of narrative patterns shows important linkages in the members' interpretation of how things are in the organization and highlights the mental ordering of oppositions (Barley, 1983) present in most interpretative frameworks: Who are interpreted as the good guys and bad ones? What do members of the organization wish to achieve and what do they expect to contribute themselves? Whereas the study of symbols seeks to understand the meanings associated with distinct things, words, situations, etc., the study of narrative patterns looks for the ways in which organizational members associate actants in the story-line(s) when picturing their organizational order.

Relations among Key Symbolic Expressions

A cultural understanding seldom takes its point of departure in a description of the organization members' world view. Rather, it approaches the world view via interpretations of the organization's various symbols. Therefore, in the interpretative process of understanding culture it is necessary to distinguish between the symbols (physical, behavioral and verbal symbols) and the more general symbolic expressions, constituted by the interpretative patterns between symbols. Therefore, the key symbolic expressions within the symbolic perspective do not all have the same conceptual status.

Key Symbolic Expressions

Architecture, rituals, myths and stories are typical pathways for understanding the culture. They are demarcated symbols which are easy to identify in the organization. They can be immediately described by the interpreter as a means of understanding their meaning. Ethos and world view, in contrast, are far more comprehensive concepts. Hence, there are fewer world views and ethos within the individual culture than stories, myths and rituals. Delimitation and description of the world view and ethos may demand numerous interpretations of symbolic expressions in order to elucidate these concepts' unique contents.

The different key symbolic expressions are illustrated in Figure 4.2. The figure shows the different types of symbols and emphasizes the more general character of world view and ethos.

In opposition to looking for a variety of artifacts at the same time as within the functionalist perspective, the interpreter within the symbolic perspective selects a few significant symbols (key symbols as described in Ortner, 1973) as analytical starting points in the interpretation of culture. By using the theoretically defined concepts to help identify the analytical starting points the cultural interpretation seeks to follow associated symbols in the further interpretation. Hereby, the interpreter can start criss-

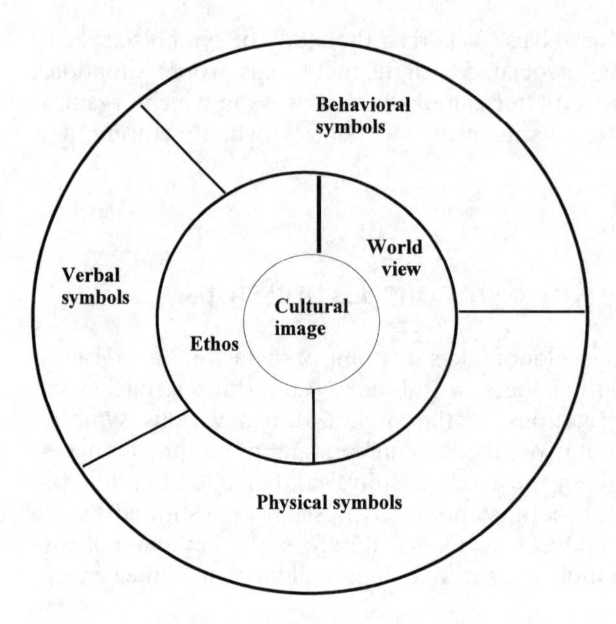

Figure 4.2. The Key Concepts of Symbolism

crossing the cultural space and achieve a much more complete picture of the organizational culture.

Associative Relations between Symbolic Expressions

In the web of culture, symbols may be related to each other by the associations of the organizational members, when they interpret things and events and turn them into meaningful expressions. These symbolic expressions may be related to each other in various ways.

1. The *contents* of the symbolic expressions may be related by the interpretive framework, shared by members of the organization. These substantial associations are expressed, for instance, when a myth serves as an explanation of actual symbolic incidents; when stories are told about physical symbols; when the use of distinct metaphors are associated in special stories.
2. The symbolic expressions are *contextually* related to each other, which is of special relevance to our understanding of behavioral symbols. The same stories are always told in relation to specific rituals, some myths relate to distinct situations or locations within the organization.

Thus, instead of only registering stories or myths as independent cultural expressions, the interpreter also searches for relationships between them based on symbolic contents or organizational context. These associated relations between the various symbolic expressions can thus create chains of meaning within the respective organizational culture, which can bring the interpretation of culture closer to images of the more general world view and ethos of the culture. This happens, for example, when the myth reaffirms the world view; when a physical symbol appears in several different rituals within the culture, which are related in the same narrative pattern; or when a metaphor used in a story seems to envision the way in which organizational members picture their world.

This search for chains of associated key symbolic expressions raises the question of whether these expressions are related to each other and provide for a further interpretation of the organizational culture – or whether they are substantially or contextually local expressions, different from the network of associated meanings in the organization.

A Methodological Model for Interpretation

The relations among the key symbolic expressions are created by the organization members' associations, when they interpret different phenomena or perform various actions. An understanding of culture in organizations thus requires further definition and increased familiarity with the organization members' interpretive processes, i.e. the associations between different symbolic constructions. Here, a method for the empirical study of these interpretative processes is suggested.

The Spiral

The interpretative process through which the interpreter empirically deliminates the associative relations between key symbolic expressions of the culture can be metaphorically described in terms of conceptual *spirals*. Figure 4.3 illustrates the idea of the spiral model. The model is completed using a random set of typical key symbolic expressions.

The movement of the spiral is neither a metaphysical nor a mechanistic process, but an active interpretive process which puts demands on both the interpreter seeking to understand the organizational culture and the data.

A prerequisite for following the organizational members' associations and interpretations is that the interpreter involves his or her own inner dialogue. The interpreter will never be able to depict the images and associ-

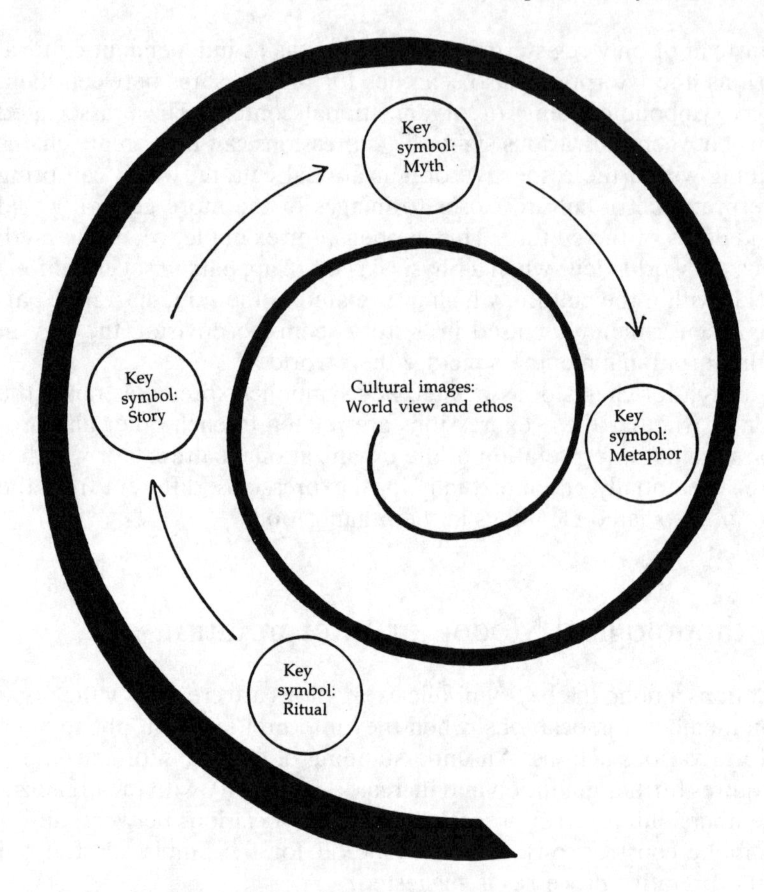

Figure 4.3. The Spiral: A Symbolic Model for Cultural Interpretation

ations which constitute the relations among culture's key symbolic expressions via a mundane empirical analysis. Via intimate familiarity with the culture, the interpreter must try to get close to and offer his own interpretation of what meaning is being created, by whom, and at what temporal juncture in the organization. In this way a part of interpretation of the culture is transferred to the interpreting subject: the person of the interpreter (researcher, consultant, etc.) becomes part of the interpretive process because one's own fantasies and inner dialogues must be involved in order to understand those of others.

The obvious risk here is that the interpretation will come to reflect the interpreter's own reality rather than the organizational culture. Hence, the effort to interpret the organizational culture helps establish the foundation for a dialogue with the organization's members, and further data collection forces the interpreter to take a position vis-á-vis the members' reactions. Ideally, the interpreter enters into an active dialogue with the members of the organization which, in contrast to Schein's (1987) clinical view, requires the use of one's personal experiences and fantasies when trying to interpret the relations among ritual, stories and world views.

If the interpretations in the spiral-model cannot be created directly in a dialogue with the organization's members, the interpreter must then establish an ongoing dialogue between his or her own associations and the data. The interpreter, to find a path from the data to the structure, must utilize his or her own fantasy, own associations and own inner images in order to turn back to the data and elicit the new meanings.

Interpretations of an organizational culture are developed neither by the researcher/consultant in splendid isolation, nor directly from the organization's data. Interpretations evolve in a dialogue between the interpreter and the organization, the latter being passive in the sense that the collection of material, as distinct from active dialogue, is generally completed before the analysis of the material commences. Both interpretative processes can be broken off if the data does not yield anything, or if meaningful images of the culture are created.

In order to facilitate insights into the associations of the members of the organization it is a possibility to apply methods which primarily seek to provoke associated interpretations of symbols in data collection. An example here is 'running commentary' as formulated by Witkin and Poupart (1985). Running commentary attempts to get the interview subjects to retell critical incidents and concrete events associated with the organization while speaking in the present tense. The method attempts to provoke streams of consciousness by assisting the informant 'to develop a commentary in the present tense on imaginatively relived events that are deemed to be of significance in the life world or work world of the subject' (Witkin and Poupart, 1985:79). The informant's focus and attention are assumed to be able to reveal 'the structure of fundamental relations in the life world of the subjects' (Witkin and Poupart, 1985:86). In the cases of this book, the interpretation derives directly out of the data.

Thick Description

Associations in an interpretation of organizational culture cannot be carried out unless the description of symbols contains a wealth of details rather than general and abstract categories. The point of departure here is Geertz' (1973) 'thick description'. Via layers of description, Geertz method seeks to elucidate the multiplicity and wholeness of a culture's symbols. The unique colors, feelings and messages in the respective organizational culture are the key to revealing the culture's symbolic patterns.

Abstract and general categories may be adequate for comparing different cultures, but they are less helpful for understanding the culture of a distinct organization (Hofstede, 1980; Hofstede et al., 1990). Thick description focuses on the rich and presumably unique features of cultural expressions. As used in the interpretative spiral, thick description seeks to map the associated cultural expressions: from myth to ethos or from saga to myth to world view. It does not try to make an exhaustive description of, say, the myth-concept in the culture.

In its richness, the method resembles that of grounded theory as described by Glaser and Strauss (1967), which is another qualitative method well-suited to the study of organizational culture (Turner, 1981; 1990). Grounded theory is defined as 'the discovery of theory from data [which] enables interpreters to develop their own theories relating to the substantive area which they were studying' (Turner 1981:225). The method comprises a comprehensive nine-phase model which typically uses interview data or field notes to gradually develop concepts for the interpretation of data and to construct theoretical implications. The nine phases can be reduced to the following:

1. Development of empirical categories close to the data;
2. collection of examples within the category until its contents seems to be exhausted;
3. abstract definition of the contents in the category;
4. locating patterns among categories;
5. formulation of assumptions about patterns between categories.

However, grounded theory distinguishes itself from the spiral model and thick description in two ways. First, the spiral model is based on theoretically defined symbolic expressions, rather than allowing all concepts to be generated concretely from empirical encounters with the organization. Second, grounded theory assumes a step-wise, exhaustive coverage of the contents of the individual concepts (e.g. a determination of the contents of myth). The definitional determination of the conceptual contents serves as the point of departure for mapping out the patterns between concepts. In contrast, the spiral model tries to follow the patterns among the key symbolic expressions in order to approach the contents. The spiral is at the same time less ambitious. It does not demand a total analysis of each of the key symbols within the organizational culture to be able to draw small cultural images, but seeks only to delimit as many patterns as necessary for formulating a symbolic understanding of the organizational culture.

Summary

The symbolic perspective focuses on the active creation of meaning in organizations and the ways in which meanings are expressed through symbols. Symbols are defined as things, actions, words, gestures etc. that represent more than themselves; the associated meaning and significance. Here, the symbolic perspective distinguishes between physical, behavioral and verbal symbols, which may all be interrelated by more general patterns of interpretations or webs of meaning. These patterns between symbols can be conceived as world view and ethos, describing the organizational members' cognitive view of order and the moral view of themselves respectively.

An empirical interpretation of culture seldom takes its point of departure in a description of world view and ethos, but approaches these more general symbolic expressions via interpretation of the various symbols. In this interpretative process, associated relations between symbols and world view and ethos may help to criss-cross the web of cultural meanings.

The spiral model systematizes the operationalization of this interpretative process which is based on patterns between the organizational culture's theoretically defined key symbolic expressions. From a thick description of the organizational culture's most limited and immediately visible concepts (physical, behavioral and verbal symbols) the prerequisites are created for an active or passive dialogue between the interpreter and the organization. This helps open the way toward further interpretation of other key symbolic expressions within the organizational culture.

The methodological process for a comprehensive picture of the organizational culture consists of many spirals, each with their own associational sequence and often intersecting with each other. In a cohesive, integrated culture, the spirals will lead to wide-ranging shared patterns among the culture's symbols. In contrast, the spirals in the fragmented, insecure or confused culture will create many individualized or localized world views and ethoses (Martin and Meyerson, 1988). Whether the culture is shared, sharply fragmented or ambiguous is an empirical question. In contrast to functionalism, the symbolic approach does not assume that all organization members attribute the same meaning to the same phenomena.

Chapter 5
A Symbolic Interpretation of Culture

This chapter will illustrate the use of the spiral model in achieving a symbolic interpretation of organizational culture. The spiral will be applied to the analysis of two different organizations: a department and a directorate within the same ministry. The formal organizational structure of the two organizations and their formal internal relations inside the ministry are illustrated in Appendix 1.

In contrast to the functionalist funnel model, which contains the same analytical levels regardless of the organization studied, the precise combination of the symbolic perspective's key symbols will depend on the given organization. Thus, the choice of analytical starting points in the interpretation of culture depends on general insights into which symbols are of special significance in the organization. The chapter will demonstrate the use a single spiral for the interpretation of the organizational culture within the department and the directorate respectively. Finally, the symbolic perspective offers the possibility of studying the relationship between the two organizational cultures.

Organizational Culture in a Department

Meetings constitute essential and visible behaviors in the department. They contribute toward structuring the organization's daily rhythm and frequent meeting attendance tends to indicate a higher position in the departmental hierarchy. In general, meetings seem to be significant expressions of the organizational culture, but especially the weekly meetings of the departement's executive group hold a high level of attention throughout the departement. There are several additional types of meetings; these include meetings in one of the department's two sections, weekly meetings in most of the subordinate offices, and several routine meetings with representatives of organizations outside the department. However, none of these meetings possess the same magic and political importance as the weekly meetings of the executive group, probably because the political minister is present only during these meetings. Therefore, the study of these weekly meetings has been chosen as the starting point in the symbolic interpretation of the departmental culture.

Meeting Rituals

The weekly meeting of the executive group (i.e. the minister, the permanent undersecretary, the two section managers [undersecretaries] and various heads of office) are attended by managers at all levels in the organization participate. The meeting is thus full of traditions, and is a permanently recurring element in the department's everyday life and relations with the minister. The data used in this analysis includes interviews and observations from the executive group's weekly meeting with the minister. The meeting is described directly from my observations, and from the managers' own interpretations. From these data we can elaborate the symbolic significance of the meeting within the organization. In analyzing the meeting as a kind of ritual, we can ask questions about the culture which helps specify possible relations to the other key symbolic concepts in this case gradually constructing the world views held by the managers.

The Meeting's Permanent Rules

The meeting is held at a set time and place in the department's beautiful old meeting hall. The executive group is large enough to create a closed circle around the old, oblong table. The table is placed in the middle of a parquet floor, away from the walls.

The meeting appears to be informal in the sense that most participants come empty-handed. No formal agenda is distributed, and only occasionally do participants come with files, notes, paper or pencils. Papers usually consist of proposals which are distributed. Some individuals may at times have a small piece of departmental paper in various bright colors used for quick and urgent messages on which they write down any questions of special interest. As a rule, however, the meeting table is bare during the meeting which is interrupted neither by shuffling papers, moving pens, or clinking coffee cups, coffee being served only rarely, following the minister's wishes.

As the meeting starts each participant takes their permanent seat. The permanent place of the permanent undersecretary of state is alongside that of the minister. The two section heads sit directly across. The minister's seat at the end of the table remains empty as the minister arrives 15 minutes later. The other participants also sit at permanent places. The meeting thus opens with a strong traditional ritual for where each person sits. The visible message is primarily that the top managers sit 'at their end of the table' next to the minister.

The meeting situation is strictly structured, having evolved into a fixed sequence of events. The first 15 minutes are conducted by the permanent undersecretary of state and typically consist of several short messages and all kinds of 'practical questions' considered necessary in the department's task performance. These may include, for example, information about the establishment of new task force groups, addressing the procedures in the formulation of official documents, or soliciting volunteers for participation in advanced training courses.

At the minister's arrival the leadership of the meeting changes and the meeting is now conducted by the minister. The minister may discuss certain important political events since last week's meeting, ask for information on ongoing matters in the ministry, respond to questions, and ask for background material in connection with forthcoming meetings or negotiations, and ideas for discussion in current debates. Here the minister directly addresses the manager responsible for the matter at hand, allowing the managers to advance their own issues. While a manager responds to the minister, the other managers do not interfere. They avoid each others' areas of competence and when they do become involved only a vague verbal interaction occurs using very general or complicated (technically unclear) questions. Thus permanent rules for how one speaks at the meeting have evolved.

There is a great difference between how much the individual managers express themselves: some become involved in dialogue with the minister during each meeting and may discuss several cases, while others are only rarely involved. There is here a marked difference between the 'speaking time' by the two heads of the legal offices and the other managers. The heads of the legal offices typically speak the longest, while other managers, like the heads of the planning office and of the statistical office, may attend several meetings without participating in the discussions. The visible difference in activity at the meeting is not indicative of any difference in task involvement or in daily workloads. Rather, it indicates that one answers when asked and does not try to project oneself too forcefully. One particular 'deviant' at the meeting tends to ask rather provocative, though relevant, questions to others. Other, minor deviations from the general holistic impression include brief side remarks, jokes or quickly told stories. The meeting ends with the minister asking the individual managers, according to seniority, if they have anything to add. There is seldom anyone who asks to speak. The minister does not recapitulate or conclude the discussions, but at times one of the participants may remark on the status of certain ongoing cases.

The approach at the meeting is characteristically administrative. The meeting is primarily a forum for updating and for mutual orientation about the current administrative situation of various matters. Problems are presented and solved within the existing administrative framework, while there are seldom any questions raised as to the suitability or desirability of these frameworks.

The general impression is of a constricted and pressured atmosphere where most of the participants maintain a subdued presence. The constricted mood seems to be associated with the presence of the minister and top managers; meetings without them seem to be more relaxed and often lead to conversations across the table. The constricted atmosphere may also be connected to the meeting's many small rules of conduct. The meeting contains a myriad of minute, unwritten rules for:

1. Placement around the table;
2. when one should speak;
3. how one should speak;
4. topics one may discuss, which can also be seen as a ritual for how one relates to problems connected to others' areas of competence or turf.

Inasmuch as the various top managers are very different both as individuals and in their daily leadership styles, it seems strange that there is so little deviation from the meeting situation's stated rules. In the daily life of the individual offices, the executive group includes managers who emphasize quite different aspects, e.g. correct case management; policy-making, system- and control effectiveness, maintaining a healthy atmosphere in the office or various forms of modern management. The socialization imposed by the meeting ritual seems so strong that there occurs only a minor deviation from the conformist, polite, minister-oriented behavior which demands that managers do not exceed their respective domains. The greatest differences involve whether one is 'on stage' being actively engaged in the interaction with the minister or whether one plays the role of the passive and silent spectator.

Interpretations of Ministerial Meetings

The weekly meeting is subject to strict rules for how the participants ought to act in the meeting situation, but take on a ritual character via their symbolic significance, and especially via the way section and office managers regard the meeting.

The managers state how the minister meeting originated in order to integrate the quite diverse members of executive group serving directly under the minister. Since the time of minister 'X', the meeting has also included the minister, and this is the only occasion when all the office and section managers and the minister come together. The managers place great emphasis on being able to ask the minister questions and interpret political views independent of the permanent undersecretary of state. They emphasize that it strengthens their own effectiveness *vis-á-vis* their own subordinates and offices if they can refer to what the minister said. The meeting ritual is thus elevated as a means of emphasizing the minister's importance; it is a symbol of the staff member's privileged access to the minister; and it symbolizes a special *élan* in the department because it emphasizes the department's unique position in having regular and direct contact with the minister herself.

The managers emphasize that the main function of the meeting is 'to get a feeling for how the minister wants things to run'. It is emphasized how difficult it is to interpret the minister's political signals and messages. A correct interpretation is said to require long experience in dealing with ministers and a frequent contact with the minister. However, in interpreting the minister's messages, the managers maintain their distance to her. To ask questions of the minister about the contents of the signals is taboo and is expressed in frequently used expressions such as, 'if the minister would just say what she wants...', or 'it is a question of feeling [what she wants to say]'. The taboo on having the minister specify her exact wishes helps nourish an ongoing interpretative activity where the managers of the department become the minister's 'oracle' towards subordinate organizations and organizations from the environments.

The managers accord the minister with unique, hidden characteristics which necessitate a special ability to decipher her political wishes; this is the department's 'calling and devotion' to carry out this interpretation by constantly refining the skills of 'listening to the minister'. The managers detect signals, sense the minister's spirit and interpret the minister's messages. After having evaluated and analyzed its interpretation the managers make the correct presentation of the minister's will which is then taken for granted in all of the organization until new signals from the minister point in other directions.

The minister's presence at the meeting thus casts an uplifting aura of status over the executive group and draws attention away from the more mundane restrictions of the meeting situation. The minister is the collective reference point for power and for understanding the political world. It is the minister who delivers the secretive hints and unspoken messages which make the meeting situation meaningful.

Distance to Everyday Life

The department's Monday meetings can also be interpreted as a ritual process, and more specifically the meetings have strong similarities with a 'rite of passage' as elaborated by anthropologists (Turner, 1967a; Trice and Beyer, 1984; 1993). The rite of passage denotes changes in the social identity of an individual which occur during the life cycle, or entrance into a new social group, such as admission into a monastic order, joining the army, a wedding, or admission into an elite group (Trice and Beyer, 1984:657; 1985; Turner and Turner, 1978; Turner 1967b). Rites of passage can be divided into three phases: the phase of separation creates distance to the individual's former role, the transition or liminal period between the two identities, and the incorporation phase which confirms and stabilizes the individual's new identity. The classical rites of passage are formulated at the individual level but are used here at the organizational level because the phases of the ritual are enacted collectively by the managers (Schultz, 1991). However, opposed to the rites of passage these managers do not change identity permanently when entering the meeting. Therefore, the sequence of rites are labelled 'rites of transition' in order to stress the ongoing transitional process rather than the passage from one permanent state of mind to another.

Let us apply the 'rites of transition' analysis to what takes place at a normal Monday meeting of the executive group.

1. *The separation phase: distance to everyday life and creation of entry into a new situation.* At the entrance to the Monday meeting the symbols of everyday life are put aside by entering into an 'empty handed' meeting situation. Everyday life in the department is characterized by paper: files, notes, speeches, minutes, piles of documents on the desks of most section/office managers. At the entrance to the meeting this most important symbol of the daily routine is put aside, and the situation changes to one of oral communication mode, where all participants meet as equals.

The minister does not participate in the first 15 minutes of the meeting which marks a ritual space for the transition from everyday life's strict role divisions to the egalitarian '*communitas*' of the meeting situation. Many signs during the first 15 minutes indicate that involvement in everyday life and its daily conflicts has not been completely left behind: the participants are more relaxed, i.e. more prone to discuss everyday problems and conflicts, just as one can better identify attitude and status differences among the various offices. The managers talk about how the 'system' (the department) works for the time being and what new demands on their task area may be predicted in the near future.

2. The transition phase: the ritual's special form and contents is enacted. The minister's arrival marks the transitional phase where the rules of the game show themselves at their full strength. Conformity dominates the picture, and the problems of everyday life are left behind. The marked differences within the executive group disappear and are replaced with a shared, empty-handed 'ritual equality' *vis-á-vis* the minister. At the same time a new 'stage' commences, where the distribution of roles, props and the script becomes different: the executive group is socialized into being 'the leadership collective' *vis-á-vis* the minister, to whom no one acts as leader.

The distribution of roles and tasks is strictly disciplined and tradition-bound, and seems to have its roots in the department's history. The extreme case-oriented approach, the legal office's very visible presence, the looking over the shoulder toward the Parliament, and the lack of cross-table dialogue between the managers express a simplified and conflict-free picture of a bygone department, quite different from the current turbulence which characterizes the ministry's tasks, and the conflicts among different task traditions of the various sections and offices. The ritual phase distinguishes itself in many ways from the social structure and tasks of everyday life. Talking about everyday life and everyday problems during the meeting is taboo, which for many managers create an impression that what happens at the meetings is not relevant for their own office – even though they spend much of their energy on interpreting the minister's winks and messages.

3. The incorporation phase: the ritual is concluded and there occurs a transition from the ritual setting back to everyday life. The phase of incorporation is rarely visible in the meeting room itself. It consists of the small talk in the hallways and offices which usually takes place after the meeting ends. Here the meeting's subjects are translated back into everyday life concerns: the roles are again broken up and the group of leaders retreats back into their 'familiar niches' and everyday roles. The files on their office-table are picked up again and the managers start working on the solutions to present tasks.

The various phases of the meeting ritual symbolically create the distance to everyday life within the department and enable the managers to celebrate the symbolic significance of the secretive deciphering of the minister's signals and messages. In this sense, the ritual 'puts a lid on the witch's brew of daily life'. The lid is put on by marking distance to everyday life and by offering a disciplined and tradition-bound symbolic conformity during the transition phase of the meeting as an alternative to a much more unpredictable and conflictful everyday life.

The rites of transition help explain what takes place at the meetings. The rites reflect the symbolic equality and integration which takes place among the managers at the meeting. The managers are separated from everyday life and establish a shared equality devoid of contents. The ritual can thereby create the simultaneous experience that something is happening during the meetings due to the minister's presence at the same time as everything appears normal in everyday life. The rituals create the experience of a continuity and inconquerability in the departmental traditions, at the same time as there occurs a contact with the wide-reaching domain of the political world.

A Further Cultural Interpretation

The purpose of interpreting a meeting ritual in the department is to both understand the ritual's special significance and to allow it to help lead us forward toward a more rich conception of the department's organizational culture by looking for associated symbolic expressions.

Within the context of the meeting the participants' attention in the ritual is clearly focused on the end of the table, where the minister, the permanent undersecretary of state, and two section managers are located. Also, in their interpretation of the meetings, the managers conceive the minister as the meaning-creating center who has both the connection to the world outside and is the ultimate leader of the organization. Thus, by addressing the associated interpretations of the minister among the managers the ritual provides additional pathways toward raising new questions in the understanding of the department's organizational culture.

Behind the ritual's predictable and conformist character are perhaps several precise perceptions among the managers as to how the minister should best be dealt with. Therefore, it may be useful to discuss the managers perceptions, and especially those of top management, of the tasks related to the minister. The enactment of the minister's significance seems linked to the managers in that their presence and symbolic conformity in the meeting situation affects the minister's significance in the ritual.

Here we focus on questions in relation to the (top) managers' perceptions of how tasks should be resolved in relation to the minister. The criteria for our choice is that the top managers in the departmental hierarchy set the framework for daily operations, and that the envisionment of the tasks related to the minister are essential in understanding how the managers picture the way things are within the department. In everyday life the differences between the various office managers are immediately visible; however, the conforming behavior at the meetings and the shared interpretations of their symbolic significance argues for a deeper understanding of those mechanisms which despite differences between tasks and personal style maintain the meeting ritual in a position of restrained conformity.

Myths and Tradition

In general, the tasks related to the minister are described by the managers, and especially stressed by the top managers as equivalent to being the minister's sparring partner. To be the minister's sparring partner is not connected to special conversations between the managers and the minister or to any specific tasks. The sparring partner task is but an expression for the minister-orientation which the managers generally utilize in order to fulfill their roles as leaders.

Old Traditions of Interacting with the Minister

The managers emphasize that there is an old tradition in the ministry for a very few meetings to take place between the top managers and the minister alone. The office heads typically participate in conversations with the minister, also on a daily basis. Thus, the sparring partner task is carried out by the extensive delegation to individual office heads; the individual managers themselves present and discuss their cases with the minister. The delegating of tasks, however, does not include the substantial issues of the tasks to the same degree, because the top managers, according to several office managers, immerse themselves in the cases. One office head, for example, emphasizes, 'that the office head could not dream of going further with an idea if the top managers did not like it', whereas another manager states that 'nothing is worse than executing new initiatives, for example, without backing from the top managers'.

Myth: What Ministers Take an Interest in

Updating the minister on a daily basis is explained by the managers according to the minister's interest for 'here-and-now' tasks. Here-and-now tasks are claimed to have the minister's interest, in contrast to the great visions. The managers relate episodes where attempts to establish visionary committees and councils failed because of lack of political interest. No minister wants to hear of such long-term commitments. In the world of ministers, the managers stress, it is a waste of time.

Previous experiences thus form the basis for a myth that the minister is only interested in here-and-now tasks, where the opposition to here-and-now tasks is tasks that are far-fetched, too future-oriented, and divorced from reality. These tasks and proposals behind them are expected by the managers to die a natural death due to the ministers here-and-now preferences. Thus, the daily understanding of tasks is influenced by a myth about what the minister is interested in based on perceived experiences with several previous ministers: The ministers are people who think concretely and who need to show themselves as here-and-now persons in order to avoid mistakes in individual cases.

Myth: What once Solved Problems...

Assuring that relations with the minister function properly, it is essential that 'the house runs smoothly'. This means that tasks are resolved with professional competence and on time. The top leaders thus see their main daily task as that of keeping the house running. A smooth running house has been the thread in the managers' administration of tasks, since the present top manager was brought in from a directorate in order to create 'peace and quietness' in a department that at the time was chaotic and ridden with conflicts. According to the ways things are told among the managers, too many attempts to realize modern management almost ruined the department and several political disasters were about to happen due to the lack of administrative stability.

The experiences from that time have laid the foundation for a second myth: solutions which solved the problems before can also solve the problems now. Such solutions include creating 'peace', going deeply into the cases and pragmatically organizing the administrative routines and the task performance from day to day. To make sure things run smoothly is the top managers most important task because the only alternative possible is chaos and divisiveness. The myth creates a universe where the room to maneuvers in daily life is very small, and where stability and orderliness is the only possible alternative to chaos and conflicts.

A World of Order

The top managers' view of their tasks in relation to the minister is thus characterized by a tradition for delegating the sparring partner role, by the myth of the minister's interest for here-and-now tasks, and the myth stating administrative, case-oriented stability as the only alternative to chaos. These myths and traditions create a pattern in a cognitive description of reality which can be understood as an aspect of the managers' world view, as they depict their most comprehensive ideas of order within the department.

Their world view can be illustrated with the help of the actant-model, a tool for describing the narrative pattern among different actants. This is shown in Figure 5.1.

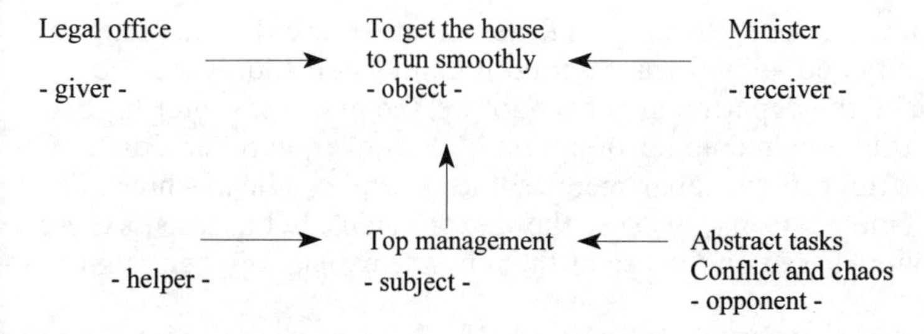

Figure 5.1. The Managers' World View Described Using the Actant Model

As stated above, Figure 5.1 indicates that the managers' principle task is to maintain the department running smoothly in order to deliver effective here-and-now service to the minister. The greatest risk and the biggest mistakes constitute the abstract, far-fetched tasks which do not have the minister's interest, or the internal conflict and chaos which are perceived to occur if administrative routines are not followed to the final resolution of any task.

The missing 'helper actant' is a result of the comprehensive delegation of competence to the office managers in the daily service to the minister. Delegation of authority implies that top management do not have any kind of institutionalized helper such as expert-staff, but stand alone facing the rest of the executive group. The managers must all be prepared to execute any kind of task for the minister, here-and-now. However, the legal offices are by far the most vital in providing the minister with here-and-now information as they are in charge of the small and concrete files which have to be resolved here-and-now in opposition to long-term tasks concerning planning and product development. Therefore, the legal offices are marked as the actant which provides the minister with daily here-and-now task solving. As a whole, the actant model indicates a stable, harmonious and administrative-oriented world view where the tasks are resolved here-and-now. Harmony is maintained with a memory of division and chaos as possible outcomes if the pattern is broken.

Metaphors: House, System or Machine

The interpretation of the meeting ritual and of the managers' world view opens a new path toward delimiting the organizational culture, where further questions to the data material must show which interpretive approaches are most fruitful. Thus again, we can utilize the interpretation-spiral model which the ritual has provided, and ask new questions of the data.

When repeating the myth that conflicts and chaos are the only alternatives to stability and administrative routines and when addressing the necessity to make the department run smoothly, the managers refer to their department using the metaphor of a 'house'. However, in other situations the managers refer to the department as 'the system' or 'the machine', just as other staff members may also use these expressions. Let us discuss these three metaphors based on the use of them by the managers when talking.

The 'House'

The 'house' metaphor paints a picture of the comprehensible, manageable, close-knit department, which is protected with patriarchal care within the house's protective walls. The department is small, pleasant and cozy. As expressed by a manager, 'We know each other and can talk together', and a staff member, 'Basically, we really like each other here in the house'. The family seems to replace the bureaucracy and is reminiscent of Weber's traditional forms of authority where patriarchalism and tradition go hand in hand. Seen from the organization's summit, the house metaphor creates an image of a patriarchal, cozy family.

The 'System'

In opposition, 'the system' metaphor introduces a new era, and it is applied frequently especially when new and more general tasks are addressed. Here, the department is 'part of the system' and sees itself as being in the center of the system. The department is perceived as if it is in the center of different systems and system-levels being the intersection for many flows running up and down through the system. But the department is also a passive center which bends according to the system's impersonal forces. The system reacts, the system acts, while messages are sent up through the system and out of it. The system is the image of the alienated technocrat who moves around in it and maintains it, but is unable to affect it himself. However, the horizon of the department is expanded to the whole system, which becomes the comprehensive concept for reality.

The 'Machine'

The 'machine' metaphor differs from 'system' and 'house' thinking in two ways. The machine contains an analytical distance to the department, the organization members stand both outside and inside the organization.

Moreover, the department is seen as a manipulable object which the machine's members can enter into and affect. The machine thus expresses a faith in rational, goal oriented action where the department can be manipulated if the correct strategy is used. The machine is therefore also linked to the political game which is 'played' actively, where people play together, where one breaks through, and where there occasionally is an all-against-all battle: the patriarch and the technocrat are now replaced by the enlightened strategist.

The use of the 'house', 'system' and 'machine' does not simply represent members' varying *labels* for the department, but also reflect radically different *images* of the department as well. Thus, the use of metaphors throughout the organization may provide a pathway for further understanding of the organization members' world views.

A Spiral of the Department

In the interpretation of the culture of the department, the symbolic perspective is illustrated via a single interpretive spiral. The spiral's movement so far is illustrated in Figure 5.2.

The figure shows how the interpretation of the data from one of the organizational culture's key symbolic expressions creates associations and raises questions of the data, which is then interpreted using other symbolic theoretical concepts.

The meeting ritual has provided a means of entry for interpreting the organizational culture, and from a relatively detailed description we have been able to interpret rites of transition. The ritual raises new questions to the data which helps define the traditions and myths held by managers' as to how tasks are handled *vis-á-vis* the minister. The traditions and myths together comprise the managers' world view: an administrative, stable and harmonious reality as the only possibility.

The department's world is described here by the managers using the 'house' metaphor. However, in other organizational contexts the managers as well as other organizational members use metaphors such as 'the system' or 'the machine'. This co-existence of the three different images of the departmental work world points toward further interpretive possibilities.

The different images of the departmental world, expressed by the various metaphors, pose questions as to the cultural multiplicity in the organization, i.e. the existence of different interpretations of the work world of the organization. The use of the different metaphors do not correspond to different social units inside the organization, as would be the case if the top managers were exclusively using the 'house' metaphor, and the staff

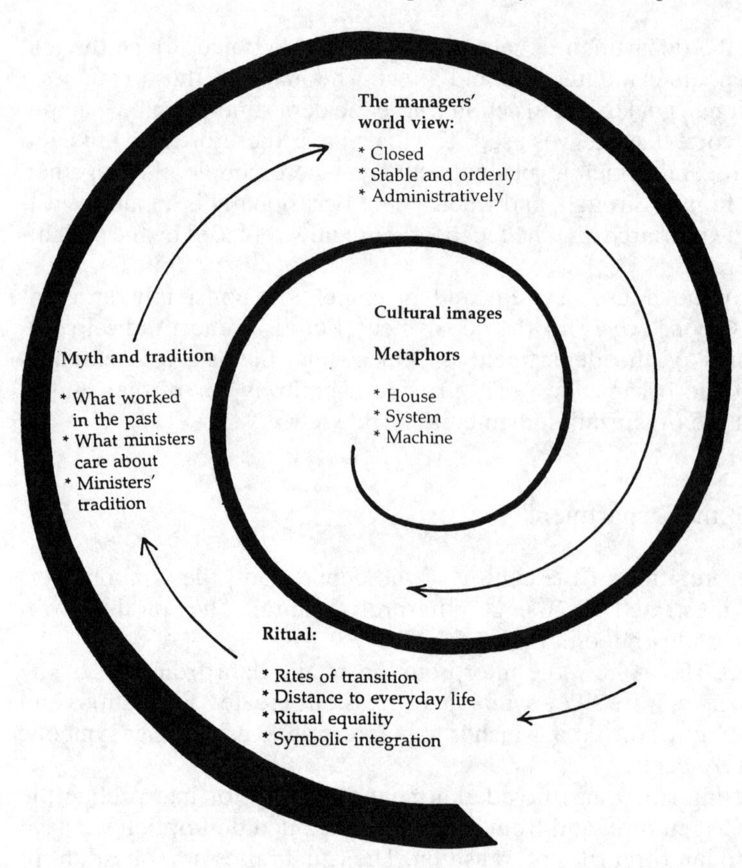

Figure 5.2. A 'Spiral' for Interpreting the Department's Organizational Culture

members were using the 'system metaphor', or only organizational members working in the political-economic sections were using the image of the 'machine'. All the members of the organization seem to use all three images of the organization and, thus, the use of different metaphors do not seem to point to the existence of distinct subcultures (Martin and Meyerson, 1988; Gregory, 1983).

The data presented here do not permit final conclusions about the implications of the various images in the understanding of the organizational culture as such. However, the spiral shown in Figure 5.2 facilitates a further mapping of the 'webs' of the departmental culture by allowing the cultural interpretation to move across the various cultural expressions highlighted through the spiral's interpretative process. Thus, in order to pursue the interpretative possibilities of each spiral it is necessary to ask whether the various rituals, myths, traditions and fragments of world view, shown in the spiral, are interrelated with one another further than the sequential associations in constructing the spiral.

Criss-crossing the Webs of Culture

The existence of different images of the work world raises the question of whether we can actually speak of a commonly shared organizational culture in the department in the sense that there exists an underlying pattern of meaning which is drawn upon by the organizational members in all situations and related to all issues. Rather, the three metaphors may reflect the existence of symbolic multiplicity, where different images are associated when members of the organization interpret different situations, events and issues.

The Minister's Household

When interpreting the needs of the minister and creating the meaningful world of order, members of the organization draw upon the associated image of the 'house'. In this distinct narrative pattern of order, where stable and down-to-earth task performance is perceived as the only alternative to chaos and far-fetched solutions, the image of the 'house' dominates. The metaphors of the 'system' and the 'machine' do not occur either in the traditions or in the myths of how to interact with the minister. On the contrary, tradition and myths both stress the managers very personal, close and considerate relations to the minister, which are opposed indeed to the much more impersonal and calculating images of the 'system' and the 'machine'.

Instead, the perceptions of a close, orderly and continuous organizational life seem substantially related to the meeting ritual, especially to the transitional phase, where the direct interaction between the managers and the minister takes place. In their perception of this interaction, the managers emphasize the close and confidential relationship to the minister when continuously interpreting the tacit signals of what the minister wants. In spite of the limited direct interaction between the minister and most managers during the transitional phase of the meeting ritual, they all seem to experience the interaction in terms of 'the minister and I'.

Thus, the image of a protected, close, and stationary department, expressed by the 'house' metaphor, seems related to issues and situations where the minister is present: In the traditions and myths concerning the minister's preferred task performance and in the ritualized interaction between minister and managers.

The System's Task-force

However, when managers and other staff members describe their relations to the external environments and to subordinate organizations during interviews, or when they discuss the organizing of the future task performance during meetings and seminars the metaphors of the 'system' and the 'machine' tend to pop up. Also, when talking about their own everyday task performance, members of the organization emphasize the 'system's' demands to the task solution and how their own task area relates to what goes on in the 'system'. Thus, among the two metaphors, the 'system' seems to be far the most dominating and therefore only this metaphor will be further elaborated.

In general, the 'system' metaphor seems to be applied when members of the organization deal with organizational issues, not related to the minister, whether the 'system' addresses their individual task area or the task performance of the department as such.

Although it does not appear explicitly from the meeting ritual highlighted in the spiral's interpretative sequence, it seems likely that the image of the impersonal and all-encompassing 'system' is related to the notions of everyday life, as it is shown in the separation phase and the incorporation phase of the meeting ritual. Here, each manager has his or her own task oriented niche, which they defend and position within the 'system'. The managers may argue about some day-to-day matters during the separation phase of the meeting, however, they all seem to acknowledge the general demands of the system from little things to important matters. Although, they interact much more relaxed and open than when the minister is present, no manager ever seems to question the necessities of the 'system' as well as the department's position on top of the 'system', which is stated explicitly when talking about subordinate organizations.

The Symbolic Multiplicity of the Department

These applications of the 'house' and the 'system' metaphor indicate that the managers may hold different images – or perhaps even world views – when they relate to the minister and their everyday task performance respectively. On the one hand, whenever issues and situations involve the minister, the image of the 'house' appears, turning the managers into the minister's trusted 'household'. On the other hand, issues and situations related to the manager's everyday task performance seem to be perceived in terms of the impersonal 'system', where the managers represent the efficient task force adjusting to the demands from the 'system'.

Presumingly, the members of the organization do not interpret the work world of the department as such according to a single image of protected order, as shown in the actant-model in Figure 5.1. Rather, they interpret the complexity of tasks, actions and issues from multiple images, which are draw upon according to the issue or social situation in question. Hereby, the members of the organization seem to engage in a social construction (Berger and Luckmann, 1966) of their task activities, where the 'house' metaphor and the 'system' metaphor help them distinguish between situations in which different kinds of task performance are approved.

Thus far, the use of the metaphors only indicates a symbolic multiplicity of the department's organizational culture, showing different webs of culture across the spiral's first sequence of associated cultural expressions. Here, the metaphors are an important reminder, that once one has reached an understanding of a consistent world view or image of the organizational culture, it certainly may not be the only one present in the organizational culture. In a symbolic perspective, the simultaneous co-existence of various interpretative patterns is to be expected.

A further interpretation of the department's culture must therefore pay particular attention to different forms of creation of meanings, and to the possibility of their developing differing patterns underneath the organization's surface of apparently shared symbols.

Organizational Culture in a Directorate

In the directorate, subordinate to the department within the ministry, people talk a lot. Nearly all the members of the organization stress that the directorate has an 'open style' where people converse across offices and 'use each other' in their daily work. The directorate has much experience with project-oriented work, committees for working up proposals, campaign groups, task force organizations and other forms of cross-organizational collaboration where it is important to talk together. 'Talk' and 'all the words' are stressed as being typical of the directorate. One hears expressions from section managers such as 'all the talk around the section', 'there is an unbelievable amount of talk', but also staff members stress that 'there is such an extreme amount of it [talk]', 'people really talk a lot'.

The impression of a really talkative organization is reinforced by my interview data; the organization's members who work in the directorate tend to be more talkative and use more words than those working in the department. Thus, verbal cultural expressions seem to be especially prominent in this organization. As the starting point for the interpretation of the directorate's organizational culture, I have therefore chosen significant verbal expressions in order to explicate their symbolic meaning. Two modes of presentation will be employed.

First, I have registered the key words and expressions which comprise the directorate's 'local dialect', and are used by most of the organization's members. Based on my knowledge of the department I have especially been looking for expressions which are different from the vocabulary of the department in order to focus on the cultural uniqueness of the directorate. Expressions such as 'the directorate', 'the department', and 'we' are used considerably in both organizations, but in contrast words like 'process' and 'seedlings' are used exclusively within the directorate, constituting instead specific, localized expressions.

The second part of our analysis records the wide range of synonyms used by members of the organization to denote the directorate's 'local actions'; for example, words like 'experimenters', 'seedlings' and 'those out there' are used again and again in the description of the directorate's tasks within local communities. In the same fashion, we list the synonyms which denote the directorate's mission and special tasks, except for the more generalized words regarding these tasks.

'Process' as Dominant Metaphor

'Process' is used by the members of the organization in diverse contexts, but it has a common origin in movement, changeability, and evolutionary sequences. Some examples of the use of the 'process' metaphor among managers and staff-members include:

Some people of the directorate talk themselves out of the process...
We have enormous chances to midwife some processes out there.
We must action on the process' own terms.
The further process...
A processual description of what is happening, but also a processual description of what comes afterwards which is, however, a weird, elastic thing.
To be part of the work process.

Process is used as a metaphor for many different kinds of experiences and ideas in the directorate. These are summarized in Figure 5.3.

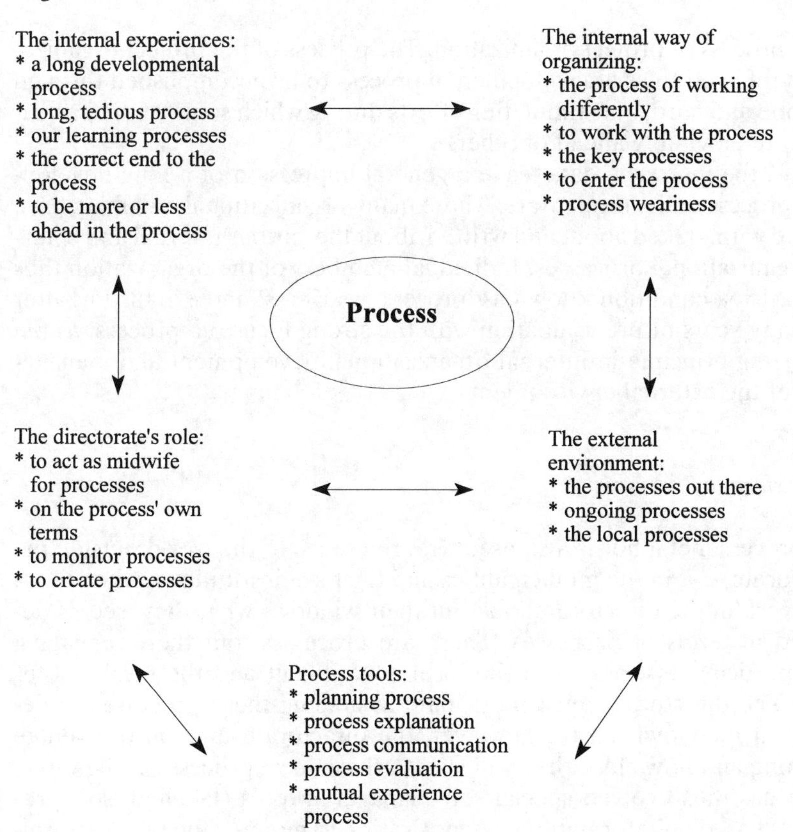

Figure 5.3. 'Process' as Dominant Metaphor in a Directorate

The Internal Processes

The process metaphor is utilized by the members of the organization regarding internal work processes. Process is used when members of the organization talk about the evolution of the directorate, where attempts have been made to develop new organizational forms and managerial tools: internally, with project organization, campaigns, and conferences; externally via the development of new, 'soft' managerial tools. These 'soft' tools are based on information and motivation from the directorate to the local governments and institutions rather than control and regulation.

Also, members of the organization use the process metaphor when evaluating the task performance of the directorate. For instance three organizational members (whose petname are 'The three Ks') have evaluated some of the directorate's experiences concerning these new 'soft' ways of organizing. Here, they especially emphasize the necessity of the various phases in the process of project organization. The process of the project organization is referred to as a developmental process to be accomplished through tiresome and hard, but stimulating efforts during which some of the participants are inevitably ahead of others.

Thus, the interview data leave a general impression of a long development process in the directorate, where many organizational members have worked with, talked about and written about the various internal and external organizational processes. Individual members of the organization thus emphasize a condition known as 'process weariness' and exhaustion after the many years of preoccupation with the strong focus on 'process' as the organizing principle in internal organizational development and management of the external environment.

The External Processes

The process metaphor is also used with reference to the world outside the directorate, e.g. in the municipalities and the local institutions: when those who work in the directorate look out their windows what they 'see' is described in terms of processes. There are processes 'out there' engaging local participants working in the local government and the local institutions. The directorate must participate in helping these processes to develop on their own terms. However, the directorate must also evaluate how long and how close they will stay to these local processes. The directorate has thus evolved special soft managerial tools (labelled 'soft processes') based on information and motivation to monitor the task performing processes taking place 'out there' in the local governments and institutions.

However, staff members of the directorate also mention the risk of being a 'process criminal' interfering with the natural development of the local activities. The process metaphor thus seems to encompass everything: work methods, involvement and endurance during the process, personal experiences, local reality and the directorate's new role. The members of the organization take their experiences with them in the work process, where they are discussed continually. New processes are set in action in order to discuss new tasks. Staff discuss how far the directorate may pursue and interfere with the processes taking place in the local municipalities.

The Metaphor as Bridge-building

Thus, the process metaphor builds bridges connecting the members' own experiences, their understanding of the directorate's new role and of the activities taking place in the local organizational environments. The internal and very talkative culture helps keep the process alive because 'talk' is both part of the process and above the process, 'metaprocessual', so to speak . Here the process metaphor leads one toward a closed, circular system. The system is defined in terms of the dominant metaphor used by the members to work through their organizational and managerial experiences inside the organization. This metaphor is then reapplied in the perception of the directorate's external tasks and for understanding the world beyond the organization. The system is illustrated by the arrows between the different applications of the process metaphor in Figure 5.3.

'Experimenters' and 'Seedlings'

A second overwhelmingly verbal universe is linked to the members' use of 'the local' referring to the activities taking place in municipalities and local institutions subordinate to the regulations of the directorate. Members employ several 'verbal flowers' for the numerous local activities which are enacted by employees of the local municipalities and institutions, but also by local citizens who have volunteered to participate in these local activities. Also, the members of the directorate use various labels in order to characterize the directorate's new role in relation to these local activities. Both localized actions and the directorate's role are described via a multiplicity of words which do not systematically refer to different groups at the local level nor to any specific types of activities.

'The Local': Expressions and Connotations

The words contain associations which tend in different directions: The expressions of 'experimenters' is used to characterize active, self-directed persons who choose to throw themselves into experimental activity: These 'experimenters', as they are labelled by the members of the directorate, may or may not be employed at local municipal institutions. The important thing is that they participate in experiments e.g. concerning new ways of organizing local institutions, new forms of collaboration between different kinds of institutions, new ways of integrating clients into the organization and distributing social welfare services. In contrast the expression of 'seedlings' characterize those cautious attempts to get activities moving, which cannot succeed without help from outside, e.g. the directorate. The 'seedlings' basically refer to the same type of local activities as 'experimenters', but 'seedlings' stress the fragile character of these activities and especially emphasize the participation of volunteers and clients.

The words' differing associations, or connotations, can be understood more systematically by distinguishing between the contents of an expression and its connotation. Thus, the members' expressions for local activities and the participants engaged are classified into expressions and connotations. I have first listed all the members' various expressions for the local activities. The expressions on the list have then been grouped into synonymous expressions, either because they reflect the same verbal image or because they seem to create the same kind of associations.

'Seedlings' and 'sprouting' reflect the same verbal imagery, while expressions of 'people on the floor' and those 'out there' tend to create similar associations in that they stress the distance to the directorate. The interpretation of these expressions derives from the context in which the different expressions appear during interviews, observation and written documents, but the interpretation is continued via the interpreter's associations. The expressions for the local activities and their connotations are depicted in Table 5.1.

Clusters of Connotations

The connotation of the first cluster of expressions concern the far, cool, horizons 'out there'. These expressions stress the distance from the directorate to 'the local', but also the local dependency of the directorate. 'The local' is within the field of vision, when the directorate from its observation post finds its telescope and looks out across the landscape in order to see what is moving. The climate can be cold and windy 'out there', when new ideas are turned down and it is hard to raise resources for new ways of organizing. But the directorate offers shelter and nourishment to the people out there. These connotations also indicate a notion of clear boundaries, held by the members of the directorate, between 'us in here', and 'them out there'. In spite of the almost solidaric shelter and nourishment offered by the directorate the many expressions of 'out there' also indicate a relief that the members of the directorate are 'in here' rather than 'out there' in the cold wind.

The connotation in the second cluster of expressions is much more fertile, organic and growth oriented: seedlings which sprout up, and eventually make a field. It is not a field of weeds but of thousands of small experimental flowers in which clients discover new opportunities and local institutions start integrating clients in new ways. The verbal flowers are re-

Table 5.1. Connotations of Local Activities in the Directorate

Expressions

a) *People on the floor*
Out and around
Those out there
The harsh reality

b) *Sprouting*
The field
The seedlings
The field of flowers
1000 flowers

c) *The experimenters*
Grass roots

Connotations

a) *'People on the floor'*
Far, cool horizons. Long distance from directorate but within the field of vision.
Round about the directorate, which is the center and observation post.

b) *'Sprouting'*
Fertile, organic growth which sprouts up and creates more and more social experiments.
A natural harmony and balance.

c) *'The experimenters'*
The self-helping activists, who are the driving forces and offer challenges in the experimental domain.

trieved from the sensitive and fragile part of nature and remind one of how each of the seedlings can be tread upon if one does not keep one's eyes open for them.

The final expressions have a more robust, craft-like connotation: the experimenters are the activists with initiative, who like tool-and-dye makers or craftsmen are the center and driving force in the local community's growth and the development of new organizational forms locally.

The Directorate's Local Role: Expressions and Connotations

In the same fashion as in Table 5.1, I have listed in Table 5.2 the expressions used to denote the directorate's local role.

The image of the directorate's role also derives from nature, where the directorate constitutes a part of nature's organic cycle; this includes metaphors such as sowing, field work where one digs deep, fertilization

Table 5.2. Connotations of the Directorate's Local Tasks

Expressions
To get things to bloom Cultivate methods To midwife ideas and processes To get the fingers right down into the earth Handpick good ideas Do field work Bring the experiences back home Help midwife things locally
Connotation
The directorate contributes to the organic and natural circulation; the directorate creates the conditions for and picks the fruit of local actions. Here it has a role as field worker, gardener and farmer.

along the way, and of the harvest where the directorate hand-picks the most beautiful flowers or fruits of its work. The directorate arrives with the generalized talents of the farmer, and the farmer's affection for the earth and his immediate natural surroundings. Even though there is a difference in the connotation of the local acts and the directorate's role, these are part of the same imagery: the natural organic growth 'out there' which the directorate is far from, but can easily see. The directorate keeps a careful watch on the seedlings out in the fields and has itself an important role as gardener in order to insure that the seedlings have the proper conditions for growth and develop into robust and self-reliant experimenters. Hence, there is no contradiction between the far, barren horizons and the local lush vegetation; the two are linked together in a single, natural organic universe where the directorate and the seedlings have mutual need for each other.

'Natural Cycle' in the Directorate

Here a metaphor is used to describe the directorate members' way of picturing the relationship between the internal and the external activities of the directorate, indicating an aspect of their world view. The metaphor suggested is 'the natural cycle'. The members do not use this metaphor themselves; rather, this is my interpretation of their world view. The natural cycle links together the members' diverse use of 'process' in perceiving the organizing and managerial activities of the directorate and their picture of the local, sprouting experimental fields. The natural cycle in the directorate's world view is illustrated in Figure 5.4.

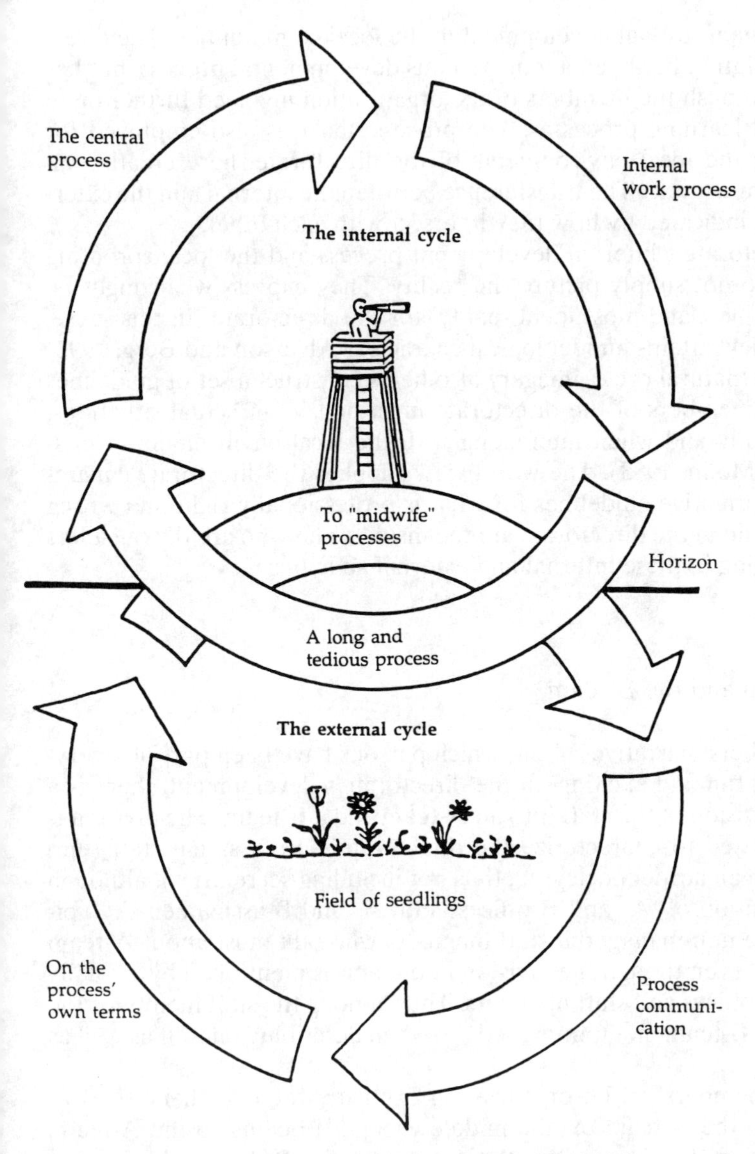

Figure 5.4. 'Natural Cycles' in the Directorate's World View

The directorate's own development and everyday life is perceived as an inner cycle. The directorate's evolution is created by new organizational forms and soft managerial tools which affect the directorate's own development in new ways and provide an avenue for understanding similar processes of organizational development in the local communities. The directorate's evolution has been a long, tedious developmental process, but has continued to push the members of the organization involved further on in the internal learning processes. The process image is also employed for interpreting the local environments of the directorate, here creating an external natural cycle. The transference between the internal and the external cycles is indicated by how they intersect with each other.

The directorate's internal development process and the local sprouting processes do not simply picture the reality. They express what might be termed the 'best and most ideal reality' for the directorate. In this sense, the world view attains an ideological character (Alvesson and Berg, 1992) because the 'natural cycle' imagery also helps construct a set of guidelines to how the members of the directorate must behave in actual situations, both internally and when interacting with the local environment (Christensen and Molin, 1983). The world view supplies the directorate's members with normative guidelines for what is professionally right and wrong and states who in the directorate are the insiders and who are the outsiders when engaging in these internal and external activities.

The A-team and the B-team

In the members' narratives about which persons have been part of 'everything that is fun and exciting' in the directorate's development, there is a recurring division of the staff into an A-team and a B-team. The division is principally used to characterize the directorate's professional staff (employees with an academic degree, thus not including secretaries), although there is mention of 'A- and B-offices' and 'A- and B-assignments'. Typically it is the non-managerial staff members who talk most about A-team and B-team, even though the division into teams is mentioned by virtually all heads of offices and staff members. Thus, among the staff members, the A-team and B-team metaphors used are when describing oneself as well as colleagues.

Several members of the organization explicitly refer to themselves as belonging to the A-team or 'the middle group': 'I belong to the A-team, and the contacts I have are all at the A-team level'. Others emphasize that 'the top management thinks that I am too rule-fixated to belong to the A-team'. However, no staff members explicitly refer to themselves as members of the B-team although the expression of A- and B-team may be used in marking one's own distance to the A-team. A-team and B-team are thus comprehensive expressions for the division of the directorate's professional staff, who cognitively describe how the staff is fragmented.

Table 5.3. Superstars, A-team, Middle-group and B-team

Expressions	Content
The leader's superstars: Approx. 10-15 persons	– 'stamp of approval' – promoted by management attention – travel to local communities – the elite of the A-team
The A-team: Approx. 30-35 persons	– participates in the larger cross – organizational tasks and teams – the glorious assignments – attends seminars and conferences – experiences all the exciting things
Middle group: 'The rest'	– the good ones who are too rule-oriented to get onto the A-team
The B-team: Approx. 20-25 persons	– members who have been working in the old directorates which were reorganized and merged in 1970 – the losers in the game – sit in the corners – no assigments or B-tasks defined as routine tasks – has lost self-confidence – no external networks

A-team and B-team are but a code for a more detailed division of the organization, which also includes the special favorites of top management and the middle group. The total picture of the A-team and B-team is described in Table 5.3. Most members of the organization speak of the respective groups in terms of size; this is shown in the table above. The sizes of the groups must be considered approximate, however.

At the top of the A-team the 'superstars' of top management are located. These are the persons who have a high degree of management attention and are permitted to go out into the field and interact with the local municipalities and institutions subordinate to the directorate. The superstars do not just talk about seedlings and processes, they experience and interact with the people actively involved in the various kinds of local activities relevant to the directorate.

The A-team consists of those staff members allowed to participate in the internal organizational processes: project teams, seminars, and all those domains where the new things are said to be happening. They receive the new assignments which have a high status and are objects of jealousy by other members of the organization. It is primarily A-team members who think and speak in terms of natural cycles.

At the bottom of the organization is the B-team, which typically consists of elderly staff members who found themselves unable to escape from their old roles or have not found new tasks in line with the many organizational changes of the 1970s. Here, formerly independent directorates were reorganized and merged into the present directorate. During this period various types of tasks and expertise were decentralized to the local municipalities, leaving members of the organization with an expertise no longer considered relevant to the directorate. However, members of the organization emphasize that it also occurs that new staff members quickly receive a B-label if they for some reason are unable to perform along the lines of the A-team. The B-team gets all routine tasks; they enjoy neither status nor 'fun' experiences. B-team members are thus envisioned as sitting in the corners of the organization loosing their self-confidence.

The transferal of staff members from one office to another is named by many staff members as one of the situations where the labelling becomes most visible. Some heads of offices cast a veto against certain persons in the B-team and 'trade them off'. This leads some people to observe that

> once in a while it becomes clear that these human trades take place, it is something one hears all around the directorate.

Finally, there is a more diffuse middle group whose members are too rule-fixated to be on the A-team, but are nevertheless not classified as belonging to the B-team. The middle group consists apparently of persons who have not given up trying to fight their way onto the A-team as well as those who have resigned themselves to a position in the middle group. The middle group also uses some of the significant expressions of the A-team activities like 'experimenters, seedlings and long and tedious processes', but these expressions characterize what one does, and what the directorate does rather than they describe the dominant tasks of the organizational members themselves. Here, there seems to be a great distance between the processual, project-oriented world and the daily, more routine type of individual administration of cases.

The A-team/B-team division thus seems linked to the directorate's historical development and the change in tasks which followed from the administrative reorganizations of the 1970s. Division into teams became visible with the arrival of a new executive leadership whose mission of soft management, 'upwards and outwards', experimental activity and dialogue with the local environment was launched via conferences, task-force groups, project organizations and campaigns.

Myths about Labelling

The staff members' explanations as to the origins of the A-team/B-team distinction do not refer to task reorganizations and former structural changes in the directorate. Rather, they consist of myths about how management has handpicked some individuals to 'carry forward the directorate's new development', while others have gotten the label 'impossible'. This handpicking is described by a member of the A-team as:

> The top managers want the most reliable horses to pull the wagon and therefore they select those whom they know can carry out the tasks.

This explanation of the A-team and B-team division created by the top management is maintained by several myths whose main messages are that it is primarily the top leaders who do the labelling, and that it is practically impossible for the members of the organization to escape being labelled and especially impossible to shift between the teams, once labelled. One myth tells of how the top managers

> stick to the usual crowd and use it like a kind of caste system. It is always the solutions presented by these people which are the correct ones.

The myth explains that the managers select a team of 'stars' whose solutions are by nature deemed the right solutions. The myth thus links together the notion of the leaders' 'eye of the needle' selection with a larger degree of acceptance if one first is placed on the A-team or has the position as a superstar.

The second myth relates how the leadership maintains the team positions:

> Top management chooses the A-team and the B-team. When the management receives memos or proposals signed by someone they know is on the B-team, they call up and complain to the office chief, even though the material is adequate enough.

The myth explains how management, regardless of the actual contents of a given situation, acts with 'blind faith' in its own understanding of the A-team and the B-team.

These myths describe the A-team/B-team division as self-reproducing: regardless of what staff members do, they cannot shift between teams, e.g. it is deemed almost impossible to advance from the B-team to the A-team and there is said to be a very wide tolerance for failures once located at the A-team making it difficult to be excluded from the A-team as well. These myths among staff members that A- and B-teams originated because of the top management therefore contribute toward sustaining a belief among the staff members who say that the division into teams is independent of the contents and quality of actual work performance: it doesn't matter because one is already labelled.

The A-team and B-team is thus an expression of the division of the organization which is frozen and self-reproducing. Several A-team members of the organization emphasize the division as a considerable problem among the professional staff members and stress that they point out to their superiors the necessity of trying to include the B-team. The same A-team members, however, are also bearers of the myths about why it is very difficult to escape from the labelling in daily life.

A Cultural Pattern: A Conceptual Map

The metaphors of process and natural cycle, together with the A-team and B-team create a cultural pattern which can be envisioned as a map of the directorate's professional staff. This cognitive landscape is illustrated in Figure 5.5.

The map is drawn on the basis of the various types of internal and external process activities which are linked to the distinctions between superstars, A-team, middle group and B-team. These linkages between the kind of process activity performed by an organizational member and the member's position on a team are maintained by the myths explaining how the managers place staff members on one or another team according to whether they are able to participate in the activities of the internal and the external process cycle.

Figure 5.5 shows the exclusively outward-looking activities of the superstars illustrated with the arrows pointing outwards towards the organizational environment. The way in which the A-team 'thinks, talks and acts' within the cycle is illustrated with a fully drawn cycle symbol, showing their participation in the internal process activities. The symbol in the middle group is drawn with dotted lines in order to show that the middle group speaks but hardly conceives and behaves in accordance with the strong process orientation of the cycle. Finally, the B-team is located at the bottom of the pyramid, being occupied with what is labelled as 'routine hairsplitting'. The existence of the A-team and the B-team is closely related to the various types of new and old tasks of the directorate, however, the placement of the individual members of the organization is explained by the myths of top management's labelling. Thus, the top management of the organization is not included in this cognitive map of the professional staff, but rather serves as the mythological condition for its existence.

The map keeps itself within the framework of the classical bureaucratic pyramid because the members' division into superstars, A-team, middle

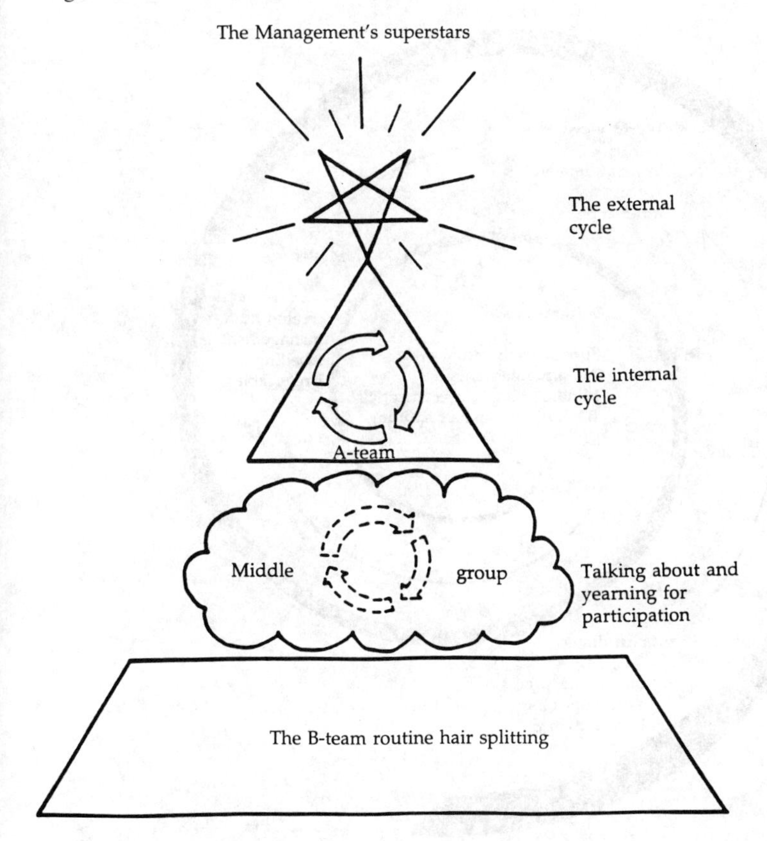

Figure 5.5. Conceptual Map of the Professionals of the Directorate

group and B-team expresses a classical 'frozen' pyramidal mode of thinking.

A Spiral of the Directorate

Similar to our discussion of the department, the organizational culture of the directorate is indicated using a single spiral. The spiral, taken from the 'local dialect' in the directorate has followed its own movement, as illustrated in Figure 5.6.

The local dialect of the directorate serves as the point of departure in the interpretation of the organizational culture. The directorate's local dialect has a distinct cultural meaning in terms of metaphors and connotations, but these verbal expressions seem also associated with a metaphor

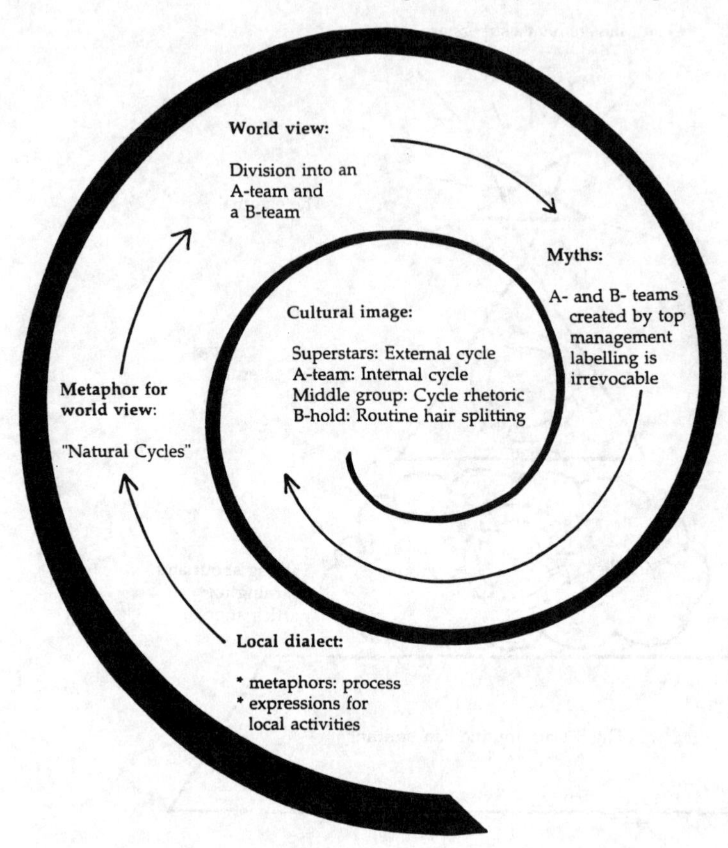

Figure 5.6. A 'Spiral' for Interpreting the Directorate's Organizational Culture

for the members' world view: the cycle of nature. This world view not only describes the organizational members perception of the internal and external processes of the directorate. It also constitutes the ideological guidelines for the 'best and most ideal reality' for the directorate. In this way we discover a second aspect of the world view of the professional staff: the division into those members of the organization which enact the right activities and those members of the organization which enact the wrong ones, i.e. A-team and B-team.

The focus on the A-team and B-team is associated with the myths which explain the origin and the maintenance of the division between the A-team and the B-team: the division, which has been created by the top management, is self-reinforcing and unalterably 'frozen'. The individual staff members cannot 'change teams' through their own performance but only due to being chosen by the top management. Finally, the linkages between the distinction between internal and external processes, as pictured by the natural cycle, and the division between A-team and B-team are drawn in a conceptual map of the professional staff of the directorate.

This map indicates the simultaneous existence of a shared recognition of these internal divisions of the staff members of the directorate and the different daily world views that each of these divisions hold. These seemingly cultural differences may be further explored by an attempt to map the 'webs' of the directorate's culture by allowing the cultural interpretation to move across the various cultural expressions highlighted through the spiral's interpretative process. Here, it should be explored whether the various metaphors, myths and fragments of world views are interrelated with one another further than the sequential associations in constructing the spiral.

Criss-crossing the Webs of Culture

Among the professionals the map describes the shared metaphor of the A-team and the B-team and the consensus concerning the status and size of each team. The descriptions of each team and the kinds of tasks team members are allowed to perform seem to be acknowledged, although in different ways, by all professionals in the organization. Thus, both the labelling and the perceptions of teams, as shown in Table 5.3, and the metaphor of 'natural cycles' envisioning the various kinds of tasks contribute to the members overall image of the directorate.

Differences in World Views

However, the map, shown in Figure 5.5, also stresses the differences in the daily world views among the various teams and groups. The superstars seem to picture the organization in terms of the external environments: the 'seedlings' and all the activities 'out there'. Most members of the organization use these verbal expressions as part of the local dialect, but only the superstars experience the 'seedlings out there' as part of their work world and, thus, as a profound image of their world view. In opposition, the A-team is experiencing and conceiving the organization as ongoing internal processes. The process metaphor first of all relates to the way in which A-team members picture their work world, imagining themselves as important catalysts in the internal processes of the directorate.

The world views of the superstars and the A-team are both associated to the myths about how top management selects members of the organization for the various teams, making it impossible to shift between teams on one's own initiative. To the superstars and the A-team members these myths symbolize the high quality of their own contributions to the directorate's new development, although they regret the consequences to other members of the organization. However, the myths of labelling maintain their position as 'reliable horses' pulling the external and internal processes of the directorate.

The group having the most troubles with the myths of labelling seem to be the middle-group, whose members seem to acknowledge the explanations provided by the myths when evaluating their own opportunities in the directorate, although they suffer from the caste system maintained by the myths. Furthermore, the middle-group is having difficulties in picturing themselves in the organizational landscape. They are trying to buy into the expressions and behavior of the A-team, but are excluded from the tasks necessary to do so. Thus, the middle group is somehow squeezed between the dynamic development of the A-team and the routine hairsplitting of the B-team.

Few organizational members refer to themselves as B-team members, as well as they don't relate explicitly to the myths about labelling. However, based upon numerous characteristics made by other members of the organization, the B-team members may be identified by the kinds of administrative task they perform and their distant relations to the new development and new local dialect of the directorate. Even though B-team members come across the process metaphor, the 'seedlings' or the 'experimenters' in the descriptions of their task performance, their perceptions seem far more dominated by legal and administrative expressions, motivating the characteristic of B-team members as dealing with routine hairsplitting. But also B-team members seem to share the image of those 'out there' opposed to us 'in here' in that they, as they talk about their administrative task performance in terms of what is being done 'in here' to provide help and opportunities to those 'out there'.

The Symbolic Multiplicity in the Directorate

In opposition to the symbolic multiplicity of the department, the members of the directorate do not seem to share interpretations, differing in relation to various issues and situations. If such interpretative multiplicity were to exist within the directorate, the members of the organization would interpret similar differences between external and internal processes, myths and local dialect. Rather, the various teams and groups seem to differ in the experience and perception of their work world, facilitating different images of the directorate's task performance and their own contributions here.

These differences point in the direction of several subcultures, defined as distinct social units with each their own organizational culture (Gregory, 1983; Pedersen and Sørensen, 1989; Louis, 1983; Martin and Meyerson, 1988). But several cultural characteristics suggest a shared acknowledgement of the overall mapping of the organization into various teams and groups, as well as parts of the local connotations seem to penetrate all teams and groups. Also, the myth about labelling are recognized by most members of the organization, although their interpretations of its implications differ significantly. Thus, compared to the notion of subcultures within cultural theory, the boundaries between the teams are blurred, just as cultural differences seem to originate from different interpretations of one's own task performance and opportunities within a widely shared map of the organization.

An interpretation of the symbolic multiplicity of the directorate as different subcultures overemphasize the differences in world views between superstars, A-team members, etc. and underestimate the shared acknowledgement of a fragmented organization. Instead, the co-existence of interpretative similarities and differences between the organizational members should be stressed, leaving on the one hand an image of the cultural mapping of the organization and on the other hand different interpretations of the implications and maintenance of this mapping.

Cultural Interfaces between the Department and the Directorate

So far we have interpreted the organizational culture of the department and the directorate as two autonomous organizations. The organizational culture has been derived from the experience of the members of the organization within the boundaries of the internal life of each organization. The risk here is that one becomes preoccupied with the internal dynamics of the organizations and the infinite possibilities for associations.

The ministry's position within an organizational environment and the relationships between the department and the directorate raise the question of whether it is possible to include the external environment of the organization in the interpretation of its organizational culture. Here, the interorganizational relations between the two organizations (department and directorate) are used in our further elucidation of their respective organizational cultures. Obviously, to each organization these interorganizational relations only represent a minor part of the external environments. However, the organizational interface between the departement and the directorate is of tremendous importance as each organization depends on mutual interaction in the daily task performance.

Culture and Organizational Environments

In the study of the interorganizational relations between the department and the directorate several analytical choices have been made.

First, the organizational analytical level is limited to the individual organization, what Scott (1992) calls 'set level'. The focal organization's relations to various 'parties' in the environment is at the center. Alternatively, we might study the organizational culture within an inter-organizational field (sector area, branch, etc.) or for a specific population of organizations (departments, directorates, etc.).

Second, in the study of interorganizational relations culture may be elucidated in two different ways. One possibility is to focus on the interaction between the two units and study the cultural rules and interpretations of this interorganizational interface (Brown, 1983). Also, a cultural understanding of the interorganizational interface may contribute to a further understanding of the individual cultures of the respective organizations. Another possibility is to study the two organizations' images of each other and the ways in which these images effect the interorganizational relations. Here, we apply a sequence of interorganizational interaction by addressing a critical incident that occurred during the data collection as a concrete pathway toward a cultural understanding.

Thus, in studying the relations between the department and the directorate, we can utilize a case study of conflict between them, more specifically, a conflict over the writing of a series of booklets or brochures. We direct our attention to the situations where the department and the directorate collide. The collision is defined as relations which members of both organizations perceive as problematic. The collision is chosen over examples of harmonious or conflict-free relations because collision is the general impression obtained of relations between the department and the directorate, and can therefore help us to understand how these two cultures interact and operate.

Pamphlet Rituals: A Case Story

As an example of the conflict-ridden relations between department and directorate I describe a case which occurred during the period I was doing the field research. This sequence of events was characterized as typical within both the department and the directorate.

The Making of a Pamphlet

The conflict concerns two pamphlets written in the directorate as a follow up of a plan-theme defined by the ministerial planning system in relation to the local communities; e.g. a plan-theme might concern reorganizing public services or special efforts in relation to a special segment of the local population. The pamphlets consist of various publications which are distributed to municipalities, institutions, experimenters, etc. They represent a most important element in the directorate's 'soft management' of the local communities as they provide guidance and inspiration to the local implementation of the plan-theme. A pamphlet may comprise an introduction or follow-up of a plan-theme, advice and guidance to local organs, or may summarize experience in new methods for resolving certain common administrative problems across the local communities.

The data for my analysis of the pamphlet conflict consists of observations of meetings where the pamphlets are mentioned, interviews with members of the organization involved in the pamphlet conflict and written documentation which describes the pamphlets. The actual sequence of the conflict is summarized in Figure 5.7, where the arrows illustrate the essential relations.

Figure 5.7 shows how the pamphlet moves between the two organizations and indicates the reactions in each organization, when it receives a response from the other one. In the beginning of the process no direct interaction between the department and the directorate takes place, except for writing letters. Later, after a period of formal and indirect interaction, members of the two organizations meet directly in order to discuss the pamphlet in question and set directions for future initiatives. However, in respect to the pamphlet in question the conclusion of this meeting is interpreted differently in the two organizations, continuing the ritualized pattern of interaction.

Irritation as Indirect Conflicts

The conflict does not have an open character; it does not take the form of violent discussions or articulated conflicts between the department and the directorate. Rather, it is primarily unspoken and indirect, taking the form of irritation and frustration in each organization over the opponent's actions. The nature of this irritation includes the following:

1. The department is irritated that the directorate has delivered two finished pamphlet proposals which conflict with the minister's signals regarding length and format and without consulting the department. Fur-

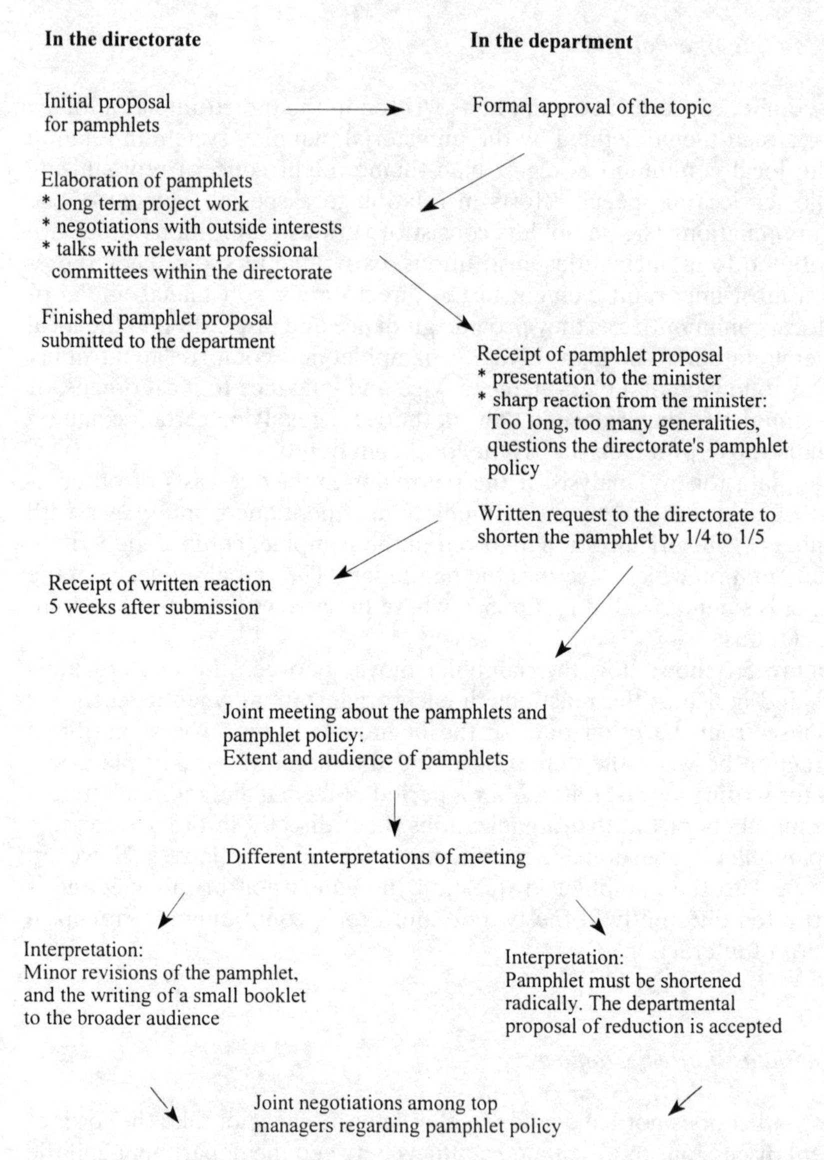

Figure 5.7. The 'Pamphlet Conflict' between the Department and the Directorate

thermore, the pamphlets have an unclear target audience and are not precise enough in their political implications.

2. The directorate is frustrated that the department, without a phone call or proposal for talks, presents a demand for a major shortening of the

pamphlet's length without providing any suggestions as to contents or any well-grounded justifications.

3. The department is irritated that the directorate, on the basis of oral negotiations, uses the occasion to avoid previous written requirements in the writing of pamphlets which the department maintains are still in force.
4. The directorate is frustrated that the department operates in a manner which reflects its own uncertainty regarding the minister's attitude about the pamphlets, but neglects to tell the directorate of their uncertainty or discuss the matter with the directorate.

The pamphlet conflict is similar to stories of other conflicts between the department and the directorate. It seems that these conflicts have a recurring pattern and create a ritualized interaction between the two organizations. The ritualized interaction consists of a relatively stable pattern of bad feelings, well-established routines, unclear communication and differences in the interpretations of what goes on. Whereas the department interprets the initiative and reactions of the directorate as attempts to undermine the minister's policy and, thus, cause trouble in the department, the directorate interprets the reactions of the department as unclear and unfair attempts to undermine the directorate's implementation of the new 'soft management' mission of the ministry, while they hide themselves behind the political power of the minister. These different interpretations mutually support each other, causing a vicious circle in relations between the department and directorate.

Phases of the Ritual

Figure 5.8 illustrates the conflict ritual, although the specific aspects of individual cases are ignored for the sake of simplicity. The arrows in the figure illustrate the essential phases of the ritual, which shift with a change in the main actor.

The recurring pattern in the ritual is that in the first phase the directorate, on the basis of a signed endorsement, submits a proposal for a pamphlet which has already been negotiated with all external interests, specialized committees, etc. without involving or consulting with the department along the way. Second, the department receives a draft version of the pamphlet, which the minister and/or department finds unsatisfactory: it may be too long, too banal, have no precise target group, etc. The department demands changes in the draft and gives the directorate a short, formal response without negotiating or involving the directorate in any more detailed considerations.

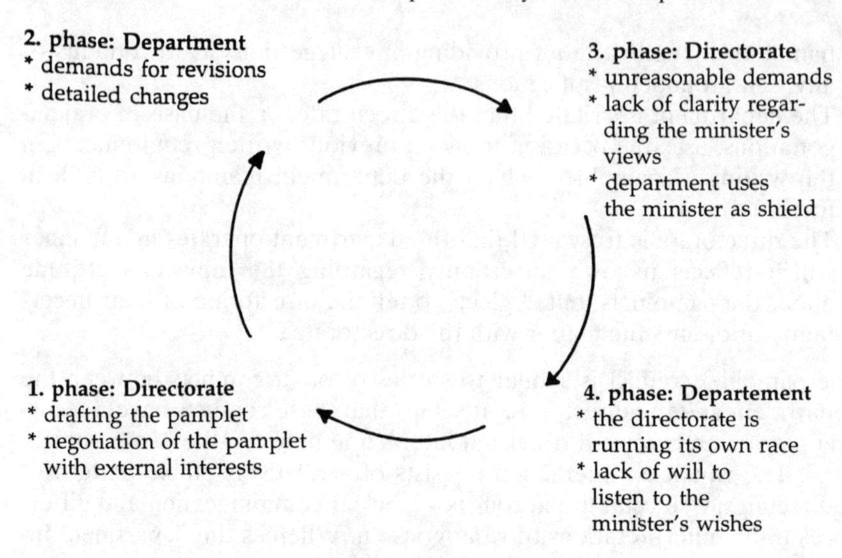

Figure 5.8. Ritualized Conflict between the Department and the Directorate

In the third phase of the ritual, the directorate views the department's demands for changes as being oriented toward trivial details, as all too vague, or as too perfunctory, saying nothing substantial. The department is perceived as using the minister for a shield, but also as trying to hide its uncertainty about what the minister really wants via empty formulations. Therefore, the directorate revises the pamphlet on the basis of its interpretation of the department's response, but without consulting or involving the department directly. Finally, when receiving the second draft of the pamphlet, the department does not think that the directorate's revised draft fulfills its initial requirements, and perceives the directorate as trying to crawl outside and run its own race outside the minister's control.

Ritualized Interface between Department and Directorate

The form of this ritualized interface between the departement and the directorate is not characterized by openness or by articulate expressions, but has a more indirect and sequential form. The form prevents the disagreements and conflicts from being clearly stated by members of the two organizations and keeps the two parts from entering into a running discussion. Instead, the ritual attains a life of its own via actions and ideas put forth by members of the directorate and department. The ritual becomes an autonomous social structure at the interface between the two organizations with its own set of rules, interpretations and mutual expectations.

These rules and expectations seem to live their own life relatively independent of other activities in the directorate and the department.

The ritual can be compared to a code which initiates members of the organization into the ritual and enables them to interpret what goes on (Toffler, 1980). The code prescribes the contents of the organizational roles and expectations which enter into the ritual; i.e. reciprocal expectations as to how members of the two organizations will perform in ritual situations. The directorate's finished pamphlet proposal, which has been negotiated with relevant external interests, would be meaningless without the expectation that the department will alter much of the pamphlet, if being directly involved in the process. Also, the department's demand for detailed revisions of the pamphlet would be meaningless without the department's scepticism about the ability of the directorate to understand, what the minister wants.

These proscribed expectations seem independent of the individuals participating in the pamphlet conflict. Thus, the ritual's pattern of reciprocal roles and rules is found at the organizational level, because the members of the organizations involved act and interpret reactions as representatives of their respective organizations rather than as different individuals.

The conflict ritual has its roots in several conflicts between the department and the directorate: the transmission of the minister's signals; the directorate's political autonomy; the target audiences for the soft forms of management. But the ritual also shows the mutual dependence between the two organizations: the directorate cannot publish pamphlets without the department's approval, and the department cannot practice the politically popular new 'soft' forms of administration without cooperation from the directorate.

The ritual can thus be seen as a way of regulating interorganizational conflicts, which keep the conflicts in place. However, the ritual also petrifies the interorganizational conflicts, because the reciprocal expectations are continually reinforced and thereby become meaningful. The conflicts are integrated into a relationship between the department and the directorate and thereby become normalized. The surprises are those relations which are conflict-free and open, where members of the two organs actually talk together and resolve problems smoothly in direct interaction. At the same time, the ritual becomes a framework for exercising symbolic effectiveness in the two organizations, in that members of one group feel and believe that they are doing their utmost and the other party is sabotaging their efforts.

The Ritual in the Two Organizational Cultures

The ritual interpretation poses new questions to the understanding of the organizational culture of the department and the directorate.

First, the interpretation encompasses cultural traits connected to the ritual itself which are common for both the department and the directorate. The most important of these are:

1. Indirect modes of communicating which are interpreted differently by the two organizations;
2. unspoken, but predictable irritation and frustration among the involved staff members;
3. conflict avoidance, where emphasis is placed on conflicts which are isolated from the rest of organizational life;
4. reciprocal linkage between an 'enemy' image and symbolic effectiveness which is mutually reinforced for both organizations, i.e. that it is the other one which is creating the problems.

The ritual comprises a behavioral pattern of its own with different origins and social consequences in the two organizations. The ritual creates and maintains two different socially defined realities, just as the impact of the ritual is different in the department and the directorate. Thus, the ritual can be viewed as a sequence of minor interactions between the department and the directorate, which may serve as pathways for an additional understanding of the local culture in the two organizations. For example, the directorate's submission of a negotiated pamphlet proposal to the department or the department's reactions toward the minister when receiving the proposal, can become pathways toward a fuller understanding of the local culture in the two organizations.

The Ritual in the Directorate

In the directorate the ritual has a strong organizational basis and plays an important role in the understanding of the directorate's everyday life. Significant organizational resources are committed to the ritual activities and the implementation of the 'soft' management are considered a major objective of the directorate throughout the organization.

The ritual events highlight the directorate's expectations when interacting with the department. In principle, the directorate claims to be eager to communicate and collaborate with the departement; in practice it does not expect a response from the department and, thus, ceases to ask for it. This confirms the directorate's own self-image or ethos as a 'soft, receptive and open-minded' organization, that is trying to develop new managerial tools and systems based on dialogue and mutual understanding.

At the same time, the directorate's image of the department as 'the inflexible, the closed and the uninterested' is maintained regardless of how the department actually conducts itself. If the department does not understand the signals from the directorate, indicating that a pamphlet is being made in the directorate, they are too close-minded and uninterested and must therefore not be included; alternatively, if the department understands the signals and reacts, they are too inflexible and without insight into the substance and must therefore not be listened.

The Ritual in the Department

In the department the ritual is on a weak organizational foundation and receives less attention throughout the organization. Only few organizational resources are involved and only a limited number of organizational members are aware of the interorganizational conflicts. However, the department's attention towards the ritualized activity is different from that of the directorate. Whereas the ritualized activity, the interpretations and reactions appear to be part of everyday life inside the directorate and therefore undramatic: the members of the department seem much more emotionally involved in the ritual, creating a dramatic atmosphere of interaction.

The most essential new cultural feature here is the department's experience of innocence *vis-á-vis* the minister when being exposed to the initiatives and proposals from the directorate.

The department's undersecretaries and office heads, in dealing with the minister's negative reaction, are quick to note where responsibility does not lay. One surrounds oneself with an aura (Christensen and Kreiner, 1984) which at a crucial point provokes an image of the 'innocent but brave department which is again burdened by the directorate's sinister projects'.

The department's lack of interest in and lack of support for the directorate's proposals becomes meaningful because, in reality, the department does not feel sorry for the directorate or the directorate's pamphlets, when being rejected by the minister. Rather, the managers of the department feel sorry for themselves. It is the *department*, which by approving the pamphlets did not know what it was getting itself into, which should be accorded sympathy. The 'poor, innocent' department now encounters difficulties in converting the minister's view into a concrete response to the directorate and thereby bringing the ministry out of its dilemma caused by the directorate's proliferation of longwinded pamphlets. Viewing itself as

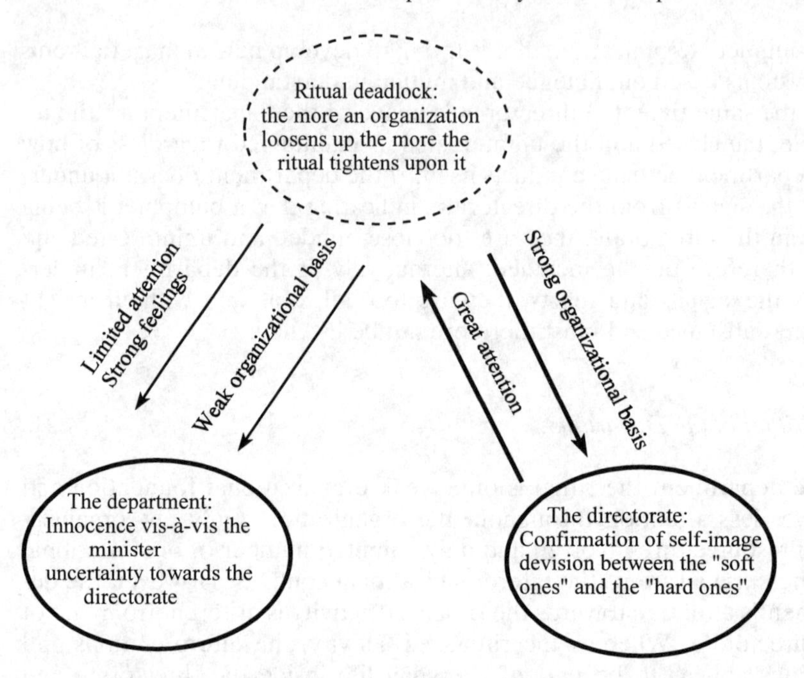

Figure 5.9. The Interface Ritual between Department and Directorate

an innocent and misused organization is very different from the department's role as the omnipotent interpreter of the minister's political gestures and signals. However, this interpretation indicates how the department, under the eye of the minister, handles uncertainty when dealing with a subordinate directorate.

The Ritual as Organizational Dead Lock

Figure 5.9 illustrates how the ritual becomes an autonomous social structure between the department and the directorate, and shows how the interpretations of the ritual in the two organizations express different cultural features of the two.

If the department or directorate tries to react in another way than that prescribed by the ritual (e.g. by taking the signals seriously or submitting materials in early drafts for comments), the other organization counterpart will be even more locked into their reciprocal roles and rules which the ritual contains. If the directorate seeks to involve the department, the department will feel even more misused; if the department tries to create a dialogue with the directorate, the directorate will perceive the departmental manipulation as even stronger. The ritual's interpretive pattern thus forces the two organizations into a state of organizational deadlock (reference). The more one of the organizations attempts to loosen the ritual's bonds, the more the ritual tightens around it.

The Study of Cultural Interfaces

In contrast to the restricted depiction of the organizational culture in the two organizations, this chapter has attempted to transcend the boundaries of the individual organizations. Our task, however, becomes more difficult, when we speak of an interpretation of what goes on between the two organizations. The problem is that an understanding of culture reaches further and further down into the interpretative layers: 'an interpretation of an interpretation of an interpretation' (after Geertz, 1973), such that the risk of interpreting and arguing in a circle increases. Also, the interpretation itself might seek to fill in the gaps in the organizational interface between the department and the directorate, generating questions of how to draw the boundaries of interorganizational interface.

However, the many benefits of the analysis should also be recognized. The description of the interorganizational ritual between the department and the directorate and the various interpretations of this behavioral pattern demonstrates that the organization's relations with its environment are an important and fruitful area for further developing our understanding of the culture concept. Especially, the pattern of reciprocal expectations and interpretations between the two organizations show important opportunities for further research. In addition, it is surprising that these examples of minor interactions can contribute to the understanding of the two organizational cultures. The general insights into the organizational culture are expressed in this ritual, but the case-story shows some cultural consequences and helps to systematize and adjust cultural insights.

Using the Spiral in the Interpretation of Culture

In the previous sections attempts to apply the symbolic perspective in the empirical interpretation of culture have been shown. In the interpretation of the organizational culture of the two ministerial organizations, the department and the directorate, the spiral has served as the guiding principle. For each organization a single spiral has been illustrated, suggesting further interpretations of the webs of culture. The point of departure for both spirals has been concrete symbolic expressions within the organization, namely meeting rituals and metaphors of the local organizational language. This concrete and delimited beginning of the cultural interpretation has also guided the interpretation of cultural interfaces between the two organizations, although here the spiral has not been carried out in its full consequence.

How to Reach an Overall Cultural Interpretation

In the illustrations of the symbolic perspective the intention has been to highlight a methodological principle rather than to reach a final understanding of the organizational cultures involved. Therefore, only a single spiral has been elaborated within each organization. If one was to conduct a more complete cultural interpretation of the ministerial organizations, several small spirals of interpretation should be made in order to add further insights to the symbolic multiplicity – or unity – of the organization.

In general it is not possible to claim that a certain number of spirals is suitable in the interpretation of culture, as it depends on the purpose and the level of ambition in doing cultural interpretation, e.g.: Is the purpose to gain insights of the overall organizational culture or to understand the interpretations concerning a specific issue like meeting behavior? Is the level of ambition to understand the culture as enacted by all members of the organization or to understand a certain segment of the organization like managers? In the cultural interpretations of the two ministerial organizations it is obvious that more spirals are needed, if one is to provide an overall understanding of the organizational culture.

In the department the spiral has a strong focus on the group of managers for which reason additional spirals might depart from cultural expressions significant to the employees (the professional staff) of the organization. Here, it is possible to select for instance popular stories about success and failure in the organization and ask whether these stories are associated with further cultural expressions, like rituals of reward and punishment. In case of gaining further insights into the world views of the managers, one may choose to address symbolic expressions more related to the interaction between managers in everyday life in order to try out the system metaphor as an overall image of everyday interaction.

Contrary to the managerial focus of the department's spiral, the spiral constructed in the cultural interpretation of the directorate relies on symbolic expressions among the professional staff with a strong emphasis on verbal cultural expressions. Therefore, in order to provide a sound cultural interpretation of the directorate one may choose to use behavioral expressions like meeting and conference rituals as points of departure in a further cultural interpretation. Also, the managers' role in the distinction between the A-team and the B-team of the organization is somewhat unclear, leaving cultural expressions of status among managers as a possible entrance to a cultural interpretation.

Above the spirals are deliberately characterized as small, as certainly not all spirals will lead to a long sequence of interrelated cultural expressions. On the contrary, some symbolic expressions may be isolated or only related to a few significations in the webs of culture.

The Methodological Principles of Symbolism

However, what is most important is the application of the guiding methodological principles expressed in the spiral model. First, a symbolic way of doing cultural interpretation is guided by the search for concrete and distinct symbolic expressions as the starting points for the cultural interpretation. Opposed to the elaborate categorization of a large number of different artifacts as in the funnel model, the spiral searches for significant cultural expressions like myths, stories and rituals and provides a thick description of the expression chosen. Here, it is assumed that the researcher has some general knowledge of the organization in advance in order to be able to pick significant cultural expressions. The selection of a distinct symbolic expression allows a thick description (Geertz, 1973) of which meaning(s) are infused into the symbolic expression by members of the organization, like the description of the various meanings infused into the process metaphor.

The thick description of a symbolic expression is the prerequisite for the second principle of the spiral: the search for related symbolic expressions. The empirical examples show that strength of the spiral is the ability to ask further questions to the cultural interpretation in order to discover associated meanings and symbolic expressions, whereas it is more difficult to point to the exact mechanisms of these associative processes. It seems as if symbolic expressions within an organizational culture may be associated in a number of ways depending on the situations in which expressions occur, the interpretations held by members of the organization and the ways in the which these interpretations are used by the members of the organization (Cohen, 1985). In the department's organizational culture the associations between symbolic expressions seem depending on situation and task activity, whereas members of the directorate use the same symbolic expressions, e.g. A-team and B-team, in different ways, creating different world views.

An Ongoing Process of Interpretation

Although the spiral may not yet be able to specify all kinds of associated relations, the ability to raise new questions in the cultural interpretation has proved valuable, facilitating a substantial understanding of the interrelated 'webs of culture' (Geertz, 1973). Opposed to cultural analysis aiming at a fixed model in the empirical description of culture, a spiral process of interpretation will probably never claim to reach a final understanding of the organizational culture.

In the dynamic complexity of organizational life, symbolic expressions may be associated or disconnected, new cultural expressions occur and old ones are infused with new meanings. Here, cultural interpretation is seen as a process which might go on posing new questions to the symbolism of organizational life. However, this notion of an ongoing process of interpretation does not disregard the importance of small spirals of cultural interpretation and limited descriptions of certain symbolic expressions. They may provide substantial insights into the organizational culture. Rather, the opportunity to add still more spirals of interpretation reminds about the complexity of organizations and prevents the illusion that it is impossible to gain a complete and once-and-for-all understanding of a phenomenon as subtle and temporary as the human creation of meaning.

Chapter 6
Comparison between Cultural Perspectives

Functionalism and symbolism were chosen among several cultural orientations as they facilitate an immediate comparison of quite different theoretical perspectives of organizational culture. However, the additional purpose of emphasizing differences in perspectives was to investigate the consequences of theoretical variance for the more practical empirical study of culture, whether it is conducted by researchers, consultants or managers.

By definition functionalism and symbolism differ in the key questions they pose to the study of culture and their key assumptions about the nature of culture:

Key questions: What are the functions of culture to organizational survival vs. what does the culture mean to the members of the organization?

Key assumptions: Culture develops when organizational members learn to solve certain organizational problems vs. organizational members creating meaning and defining the organizational reality upon which they react.

These fundamental differences have been elaborated and have guided the empirical application of the two perspectives.

The theoretical elaboration and empirical application of the two cultural perspectives showed marked differences in their epistemological assumptions about the conceptual character of organizational culture and about how knowledge of organizational culture is obtained. Also, in the empirical and more practical application of the culture concept, functionalism and symbolism led to important methodological differences which are discussed below by comparing the two perspectives. Finally, similarities of the two perspectives are discussed.

Table 6.1. Basic Theoretical and Methodological Differences between Functionalism and Symbolism

Dimension	Functionalism	Symbolism
Key Analytical Question	What are the functions of culture for organizational survival?	What is the meaning of the organization to its members?
Analytical Assumption	Culture develops through organizational problem-solving	Culture is created as ongoing con struction and reconstruction of meaning
Analytical Framework	Universal framework: The levels and functions of culture	Context specific and organization specific
Analytical Mode	Categorical: Listing of cultural elements and discovering the relations between them	Associative: Reading associated meanings and exloring the associations between them
Analytical Method	Clinical	Ethnographic
Analytical Result	Theoretical models emphasizing general characteristics	Narrative text exploring uniqueness
Analytical Insight	Diagnosis	Understanding

Differences between the Two Perspectives

In the current debate about organizational culture, functionalism and symbolism represent competing perspectives on how to do cultural analysis in organizations. The conceptual elaboration of both perspectives shows a number of fundamental differences in their assumptions about cultural concepts and their analytical application.

Theoretical and Methodological Differences

The basic theoretical and methodological differences between the two perspectives are summarized in Table 6.1.

Analytical Framework

First of all, functionalism and symbolism differ in the extent to which they define the conceptual framework of organizational culture prior to approaching the empirical field to be studied.

Functionalism operates with a universal and predefined framework of cultural levels, functions and their interrelations. Regardless of the nature of the organization studied, culture is assumed to develop in relation to specified tasks or functional areas. Additionally, any cultural study should follow the universal levels of cultural awareness: from the superficial artifacts, to the values and basic assumptions that the organizational members take for granted. Also, at this most substantial level, organizational culture is expected to develop along a set of universal and predefined dimensions. The contents of these dimensions has been developed by Schein in his most recent works: in 1991 he adds two new dimensions: the nature of time and homogeneity vs. diversity (Schein 1991:250), whereas in the 1992 edition of the *Organizational Culture and Leadership* he returns to a redefined version of the six basic assumptions, elaborating assumptions of time and space. However, the claim for universal dimensions of the basic assumptions across different organizations persists. The relations between the three cultural levels are not further specified by Schein other than to make the distinction between the analytical and explanatory processes, moving downwards and upwards between the cultural levels respectively.

The empirical study of the ministry suggests the necessity of adjusting to Schein's universal cultural functions. That is, the general functions of external adaptation and internal integration need to be re-examined and may require adjustment according to the specific organization studied. Thus, a contingency perspective (Scott, 1992) may be applied to the relation between organizational environments and the requirements for organizational survival. Hereby, the existence of generalizable functional areas or tasks, which all organizations must cope with in order to survive, is substantially questioned.

Also, the empirical application of the functionalist perspective developed for the ministry allows far more complex relations between the analytical levels of culture. The existence of consistency and inconsistency between values and assumptions, and the various effects of artifacts expand the ways in which organizational culture may work in organizations and show that the three-level framework does not necessarily imply a homogeneous and harmonious culture in organizations. However, the functionalist framework for doing cultural analysis remains based on a set of predefined cultural levels and general functions that are to be applied sequentially in cultural analysis regardless of the type of organization studied. Furthermore, in her recent work, Hatch (1993) suggests a further elaboration of the dynamic processing relating the three levels of culture and distinguishes between manifestation, realization, symbolization and interpretation.

The symbolic perspective differs from the functionalist with respect to the latter's emphasis on a fixed set of predefined categories. Even though the symbolic perspective also operates with a range of predefined key concepts, their application depends on the organizational culture studied. Thus, the application of the symbolic perspective should reflect the specific organization or the organizational context studied and may well differ between them.

For instance, whether the cultural interpretation takes off from verbal symbols or behavioral symbols must reflect the uniqueness of the organizational culture. The symbolic perspective defines a range of opportunities for studying symbolic expressions in organizations, but assumes neither a special sequence between them nor that all symbolic expressions exist in any organizational culture. Thus, the relations between the range of predefined key concepts have a much more open-ended character. The notion of culture as a unique web of meaning, being constructed and reconstructed by various members requires a flexibility in the conceptual framework and openness to the creation of unique cultural descriptions.

Analytical Mode

Another fundamental difference between the two perspectives lies in the difference between categorization and association. This difference first of all refers to the theoretical conceptualization of organizational culture. A functionalist perspective studies culture as a listing of cultural elements (e.g. a listing of a number of values and basic assumptions), categorizing each element independently of the others. Hence, the study of culture becomes a vertical mapping of relations between each of the cultural elements or categories.

This categorical way of thinking differs considerably from the way in which the symbolic approach adds meaningful contents to its key concepts. Instead of categorizing the elements of organizational culture, the symbolic perspective intends to read the organizational culture by discovering and following the meanings and interpretations associated with the symbolic expressions. Hence, the symbolic expressions are not expected to contain a predefined set of meanings that are independent of one another within the unique organizational culture. Rather, symbols are created by associated meanings that are ascribed to them by the members of the organization. Furthermore, the focus on images and root-metaphors as ways of describing the heart of the culture, also reflects the associative qualities of the symbolic perspective, as the rich and evocative character of metaphors and images depend on the ability to associate between the phenomena compared. Thus, on the one hand the symbolic perspective seeks to understand the associative links of the organizational culture studied, created by the organizational members, and on the other hand makes use of associations in the descriptions of the unique qualities of the culture.

This difference between categorization and association points to the analytical mode characteristic of these two perspectives and helps explain how to apply their central concepts to the study of organizational culture.

Analytical Method

In the application of the functionalist analytical model to the study of organizations, Schein emphasizes that a clinical method is more suitable for the analysis of organizational culture than survey research, analytical descriptive approaches and an ethnographic approach (Schein, 1991). Contrary to other approaches, the idea of the clinical perspective is to help the organization. It is dependent on the organization's own motivation to conduct a cultural analysis together with an 'outsider', typically serving as a consultant (Schein, 1987). A psychological contract is established between the consultant and the client, which is assumed to imply greater openness in the joint discovery of the cultural paradigm. Thus, the consultant must

> find someone in the culture who is analytically capable of deciphering what is going on and who is motivated to do so. It is the insider's motivation to obtain some kind of help or clarity that makes this a "clinical" rather than an "ethnographic approach" (Schein, 1985a:114).

The clinical analysis of culture can be interwoven with the introductory set of interventions. Its validity is primarily evaluated on its ability to predict actions in the organization or guide the therapeutic endeavor.

In this book, the functionalist analysis has not been conducted in terms of a clinical method and, thus, does not address the organizational processes involved in a clinical relationship. Rather, the functionalist analysis has been conducted from an external analytical point of view and has attempted to analyze cultural data using the functionalist theory and analytical guide-lines. However, the analytical challenges involved in the categorization of artifacts and values, the discovery of basic assumptions, the deciphering of the relations between the cultural levels, and so on are similar, whether the analysis is conducted by a researcher or interactively by a consultant and a motivated group of insiders.

Contrary to the functionalist preference for a clinical method, the symbolic perspective is based on an ethnographic method. The ethnographic method is used to obtain understanding and insight for scientific purposes based on acceptance from the organization studied. Thus, unlike the clinical method, where the researcher is requested by the organization to conduct a study, the ethnographer selects an organization on the basis of his or her own research and theoretical interests. Having obtained access to the organization, the ethnographer's preferred method is to collect data (wander around, observe in settings, conduct interviews), causing as little disturbance as possible to everyday life in the organization: 'The ethnographer starts with the assumption that the organization is there to be understood and left intact' (Schein, 1987:32).

A true ethnographic study should be based on a long period (one to two years) of full-time participant observation in the organization, making it possible to learn the meaning of events and actions to the organizational members (Spradley, 1979). Very few full-scale ethnographic studies of organizations have so far been conducted; examples are Kunda (1991), Barley (1983) and Feldman (1989). Most studies are based on a somewhat shorter period of less intensive data-collection, e.g. the study of this book, which is based on data collection during a year, including weekly participant observations. The symbolic perspective is strongly rooted in ethnography and the works of Geertz (1973; 1983; 1988), but in its application to the study of organization the pure ethnographic method has blended with methods from semiotics and the social sciences, which are less demanding in terms of required presence in the field. Here, the intensity rather relates to the richness of the data material, e.g. long and detailed qualitative interviews, revealing the ways in which the organizational members construct meaning.

Analytical Result

This methodological application of the two perspectives to an empirical field produces different analytical results, which show different ways of conceptualizing analytical results.

The functionalist perspective models the organizational culture as an analytical field, specifying the contents of each cultural level and their interrelations strongly emphasizing the basic assumptions. Here, model-building is an useful method, as the universal and predefined set of cultural levels and cultural dimensions make model-building possible. Any organizational culture can be analyzed and depicted within the predefined model. The analytical use of a functionalist model makes it possible to conduct comparative studies of different organizational cultures, whether these comprise different cultures among groups/divisions, etc. within the same formal organization, or separate formal organizations. The universal character of the predefined cultural model and, hence, the repeated analytical schedule to be followed, facilitate the comparison of cultures.

In a comparison of several different organizational cultures, where the goal is to elaborate basic similarities and differences, the cultural paradigm is in focus. Regardless of changing tasks and fashionable artifacts, the cultural paradigm constitutes the foundation for understanding the apparent confusion and changeability of the cultural surface manifestations, whereas values and artifacts are rather manifestations of conjunctural, local circumstances and immediate events in the organization. A comparison is further facilitated, if the analysis of the cultural paradigm is developed according to the five, six or seven dimensions of the basic assumptions, suggested by Schein (1985a; 1991; 1992). In the former empirical analysis, the analysis of the basic assumptions has been of a more limited character, as it does not define the basic assumptions in close correspondence with the dimensions suggested by Schein, but seeks a stronger adaptation to the organization studied.

On the contrary, the symbolic perspective produces a range of substantial key concepts used in the cultural study based on the organization-specific associations found between them. Instead of constructing a cultural pattern along predefined levels and dimensions, the symbolic perspective aims to create links between key concepts, showing the unique characteristics of each culture studied. These linkages between key concepts form the webs of culture that are demonstrated by creating images rather than by model-building. Creating images supports symbolism's goal of creating unique descriptions of each organizational culture and definitely appeals to the creativity and fantasy used in many symbolic studies. Thus, images are used as ways to synthesize the unique qualities of the culture studied and may originate from dominant cultural themes or special synthesizing symbols (Spradley, 1979; Geertz, 1973).

The search for the special features of each organizational culture makes symbolism primarily suited for unique case studies of organizational culture, as the unique combinations of different symbols and webs of meaning characterizing different organizations may be difficult to compare.

Analytical Insight

Based on these differences, the functionalist perspective seems especially suited for conducting what has been labelled a diagnosis of the organizational culture. This diagnostic character contributes to the ability of the functionalist cultural analysis to address organizational problems and dysfunctionality. It also indicates the preferred clinical use of the cultural model.

Cultural diagnosis, based on a precise and predefined set of analytical tools, is able to determine how the organizational culture is composed of various elements at each cultural level and how these elements contribute to the task solving and, thus, the survival of the organization. Hence, the contents of the cultural paradigm can be evaluated on the basis of the demands for external adaptation and internal integration, that are imperative to organizational survival.

Although, it has been strongly argued in this book that the specific task areas should reflect the organization studied, the absence of some task areas, defined as the lack of cultural values and assumptions coping with these tasks, may indicate serious problems for the organization's survival. Also, within a functionalist framework strong inconsistent relations between either the basic assumptions or between basic assumptions and values may indicate severe instability and, thus, dysfunctionality, of the organizational culture. These inconsistencies may obviously threaten the long-term stability and the consensus of the organizational culture, as they leave the members of the organization with uncertainty in relation to 'the correct way to perceive, think and feel' (Schein, 1985a:9). However, it may also be argued, that the cultural inconsistencies are functional to a dynamic cultural development, creating the tensions and uncertainties necessary for renewing the cultural paradigm. That organizational culture may work as 'blinders' to cultural renewal has often been stressed (Schein, 1985a; French and Bell, 1990) and here cultural inconsistencies may help prevent a mature culture from becoming a source of self-defense instead of a source of dynamic development.

Thus, the functionalist diagnosis of the organizational culture makes it possible to address issues that

> have to do with examining strategic options, the potential resistances to change that a turnaround may encounter, the need to examine whether certain assumptions that have worked in the past are still well matched with environmental realities, the need to identify aspects of the culture that the group wants to preserve in a period of rapid change, and so on (Schein, 1991:253).

A cultural diagnosis makes it possible to estimate culture's contribution to organizational survival in a long-term perspective and make use of the short-term cultural functionality/dysfunctionality in relation to issues like changes in strategy, mergers and acquisitions, or the need for a turnaround.

Contrary to the functionalist diagnosis of organizational culture, the symbolic perspective seems especially capable of creating an understanding of the organizational culture based on its own conceptualizations and meanings. The symbolic perspective aims at understanding which meanings members of organizations ascribe to the organization, creating their own and distinct set of interpretations. In the words of Spradley, 'rather then studying people, ethnography means learning from people' (Spradley, 1979:3).

Thus, the aim of a symbolic interpretation of culture is to obtain knowledge, which makes it easier to understand the culture on its own premises. However, in an organizational setting, a cultural understanding may often imply an organizational response in case it is communicated to the members of the organization. An evocative cultural description may lead organizational members to reflect upon their own culture(s), thus, provoking a discussion of the strengths and weaknesses of the prevailing culture in relation to future organizational development.

Although a symbolic understanding neither explicitly seeks to cause organizational change nor holds the assumptions that the only way to understand an organization is to change it, cultural understanding may bring about substantial organizational changes due to the responses and reactions by the organizational members. However, a symbolic cultural analysis is separated from an eventual process of organizational change and does provide feedback rather than help to the organization.

In the case of this book, the cultural descriptions were in another format communicated to the organizational members on several occasions and did no doubt form an important platform for the discussion of the problems involved in a future merger between the department and the directorate.

Differences in Empirical Application

Based on these theoretical and methodological differences, a number of differences in the empirical application of the two perspectives are also found. These differences are summarized in Table 6.2.

The functionalist perspective is typically viewed as the most accessible perspective when doing empirical analysis, especially among consultants and students. Functionalism is well-defined and contains an analytical model which can be directly applied to the empirical field. Data must simply be collected and organized according to the various categories of the analytical model. For these reasons, functionalism is often perceived as conceptually attractive and well-suited for providing a quick overview of an organizational culture, although Schein himself strongly stresses the difficulties of approaching the level of basic assumptions. These difficulties are supported by the empirical study of this book.

The empirical results from doing an overall empirical study, however, indicate that functionalism is extremely data demanding, labor intensive, and thereby costly in terms of time and energy. The systemic conceptual-

Table 6.2. Differences in Empirical Application between Functionalism and Symbolism

Dimension	Functionalism	Symbolism
Extent of Empirical Analysis	A total analytical process	Many small interpretative processes
Preconditions of Empirical Analysis	Starts with predefined categories	Demands organizational insight in order to select relevant data
Data Requirements	Much data across the levels and functions of culture collected sequentially	In depth data collected incrementally
'Costs'	Very demanding on researcher's time and energy: High costs	Varied costs in researcher's time and energy: Flexible costs

ization of culture is reflected in the empirical analysis in the sense that the full-scale data collection must be almost finished before it is possible to reach any results of the cultural analysis. Artifacts and values cannot be fully deciphered until the cultural paradigm is uncovered. The data requirements for analyzing the three levels of culture (artifacts, values and basic assumptions) soon expand when having to analyze the complete range of tasks or functional areas and all the dimensions of basic assumptions. Moreover, functionalism requires a comprehensive data base: the artefact level necessitates a wide range of observational materials and archival studies. Values and basic assumptions make demands on the interview data, at least supported and validated by special motivated insiders of the organization (Schein, 1985a:Chapter 5). The study of basic assumptions also requires extensive participant observation and observation of critical events. In addition, both values and basic assumptions make heavy demands on the researcher's analytical sophistication as the analysis requires elaborate elicitation procedures in order to be able to distinguish between both the functions and the levels of culture. For these reasons, the application of a functionalist framework for doing cultural analysis may be very demanding in terms of time and energy and thus imply a high level of costs.

However, Schein also stresses that the cultural analysis may be applied by an outsider to a group of insiders, thus using the model as an exercise in a process-oriented way typical to a clinical perspective (Schein, 1991:253; French and Bell, 1990). Here, the outsider, typically a consultant, asks the group to brainstorm the contents of each box in the three-level model.

Stimulated by the outsider, the group is pushed further in identifying the level of basic assumptions. Hence, it should be emphasized that the demands for the empirical application of the functionalist framework discussed above first of all relate to the situations in which the outsider (researcher or consultant) is conducting an empirical study of the organization culture.

Symbolism, in contrast, has the reputation of being very complicated and has often been discussed in terms of its seemingly exotic or unscientific character. The rather vague conceptual framework along with the strong inspiration from humanistic concepts and methods has no doubt contributed to the expectation of complex and extensive empirical studies within a symbolic framework.

Based on these expectations, the empirical application of symbolism is surprising because symbolism in several ways tends to be easier to apply than functionalism. Although symbolism also aims to obtain a rich overall interpretation of the organizational culture, the symbolic framework is applied in a series of small interpretative processes, each offering insights into the organizational culture. Thus, symbolism provides rapid substantive results because each individual interpretive spiral contains an independent partial result which is useful for understanding the culture. The incremental character of the data collection supports the achievement of minor or partial results in that the associated key concepts direct the collection of relatively few data that promote in-depth understanding. As such, cultural understanding is created by many small, but richly detailed interpretive processes that demand less data and generate more profound understanding. Symbolism does not require any predefined full-scale data collection, but rather intends to follow the pathways associated with the key concepts that are the focus of the specific study. This is not the case with functionalism, where, for example, elucidating the value level does not contribute so directly to our understanding of the organizational culture as such.

However, the application of the symbolic framework requires a general insight into the organization, before the different key concepts for defining the culture can be selected, and before any pathways can be established. The requirements for this general organizational insight are hard to specify, as it depends both on the distinctiveness of the organizational culture being studied and on the opportunities of creating a dialogue between the researchers and members of the organization. Thus, similar to functionalism, the application of a symbolic framework may be facilitated by engaging the insiders actively in the interpretative process, here by pointing to significant symbolic expressions of the organizational culture. However, no matter what level of involvement organizational members contribute, it should be emphasized that the application of a symbolic framework requires careful consideration of which key concepts and pathways to follow.

As the symbolic framework does not contain a fixed set of predefined key concepts to be examined in order to achieve a rich and overall cultural understanding, the time and energy required to conduct a cultural analysis become much more dependent on the specific organizational context. Symbolism holds no expectations of reaching a final understanding of the organizational culture, like discovering the web of meaning which makes it possible to decipher the full range of symbolic expressions. Rather, it acknowledges that the interpretation of cultures is a never ending process, which makes it possible to conduct small and insightful interpretations of organizational culture, realizing the limitations of each cultural image, of course. Thus, the decision of when and how to end the collection and interpretation of data depends on the ambitions of the outsider and the requirements of the insiders rather than on some universal prescriptions of the conceptual framework itself.

Summary

Important differences between a functionalist and a symbolic perspective emerge from a comparison of their conceptual frameworks and the ways in which each proposes to study organizations. The two perspectives are significantly different in that one relies upon predefined and categorical model-building, listing and deciphering organizational culture at various levels and dimensions, while the other uses an openly defined set of key concepts, which, via association, forms the linkages and webs of culture, creating cultural images unique to each organization studied. The differences in the empirical application of the two perspectives are related to the conceptual differences in that the predefined categorial framework poses extensive demands to the empirical study of culture both in relation to the analytical process and to the data required. In contrast, the more openly defined associative set of key concepts requires a set of preconditions in order to be applied, but its demands on the empirical application itself are more flexible in terms of data and costs, but also in terms of the possible results obtained.

Similarities between the Two Perspectives

In spite of the important differences between functionalism and symbolism, there are a number of important similarities between the two perspectives as they have been defined and applied in this book. Recent years' academic debate and critique of concepts of culture have made these simi-

Table 6.3. Similarities between Functionalism and Symbolism

Dimension	Functionalism	Symbolism
Culture as Patterns	A pattern of basic assumptions	A web of meanings
Culture as Relations Between Depth and Manifestations	Discovering the deep level of culture makes it possible to decipher visible and espoused level of culture	Interpreting the webs of meaning makes it possible to understand the symbolic expressions as representations of deep layers of meaning

larities more obvious. In the beginning of the 1980s symbolism was to a large degree defined as an alternative to a functionalist framework (Smircich, 1983b; Pondy et al., 1983; Putnam, 1983), creating a wide range of new theoretical and methodological opportunities for studying organizations; today, however, some would claim that the similarities of the two perspectives should also be taken into consideration. For instance, recent developments within concepts of ambiguity and postmodernism have criticized aspects of the concept of culture, inherent in both the functionalist and symbolic perspectives.

Table 6.3 summarizes two important similarities between functionalism and symbolism, which are, however, not unique to these perspectives, but may be found in the vast majority of cultural studies. Nevertheless, these similarities have caused some criticism of both perspectives.

Culture as Pattern

The first similarity between functionalism and symbolism concerns the conceptual assumption that 'culture implies patterning' (Schein, 1991:246). Both perspectives tend to focus on the regular and repetitive aspects of organizational life rather than on the random and accidental aspects. The perspectives define organizational culture either as patterns of basic assumptions (Schein, 1992) or world views/webs of meaning (Geertz, 1973; Smircich, 1985) respectively, thus perceiving culture as interrelated sets of assumptions or meanings. Within the symbolic perspective, the search for patterns becomes especially significant in the application of narrative patterns, story-lines and other structural concepts inspired by semiotics.

However, the search for cultural patterns does not imply that the patterns are only constituted by consistent and harmonious relations. Within both functionalist and symbolic perspectives, it is possible to study inconsistent relations whether they occur between cultural levels (e.g. values and basic assumptions), between basic assumptions, or between symbolic expressions. Hence, organizational culture may be constituted by different kinds of pattern-relations, comprising both consistent and inconsistent cultural phenomena.

But, it should be emphasized that the two perspectives differ in terms of the extent to which the patterns of culture are assumed to be shared among the members of the organization. By definition Schein focuses on what is shared among the members of a group or an organization (Schein, 1985a; 1991:247), whereas the symbolic view does not hold any presumptions as to whether culture is shared or not, but allows for both shared and non-shared webs of meaning.

The issues of consensus and consistency of organizational culture have been raised by Martin and Meyerson (1988) in their critique of an integrationist framework that defines culture solely in terms of consensus and consistency. Martin and Meyerson suggest differentiation and fragmentation paradigms as alternatives, which are, however, analyzed within the same analytical matrix-model, including artifacts, informal and formal practices and internal and external contents themes (Martin and Meyerson, 1988:95-99). Thus, the matrix-model also allows both consistent/inconsistent relations and consensus/lack of consensus among organizational members within the same conceptual framework (Martin and Meyerson, 1988; Frost et al., 1991; Martin, 1993).

Although it is argued here that it is possible to study cultural inconsistency within both perspectives and to study lack of consensus within a symbolic framework, actual empirical studies of organizational culture have to a large extent focused on culture as consistent and shared patterns in organizations. Thus, Martin and Meyerson (1988) point to important opportunities in the study of culture, which have not yet been utilized neither within functionalism nor symbolism.

Furthermore, Martin and Meyerson (1988) add the issue of ambiguity, which is defined as lack of clarity, co-existence of consensus and dissensus forming a 'constantly fluctuating pattern influenced by changes, for example, in events, attention, salience and cognitive overload' (Frost et al., 1991:8). Martin and Meyerson suggest that ambiguity should be included in the cultural portrait of the organization. Here, the notion of patterning, especially within the functionalist perspective, may prevent a full and rich understanding of cultural ambiguity, as the complexity, fluidity and duality of the ambiguity concept are hard to grasp in the search for cultural patterns (March and Olsen, 1976).

Culture as Relations between Depth and Manifestations

Within both perspectives, the cultural patterns are located at the depth of the organization. Schein explicitly describes the pattern of basic assumptions as 'the deeper levels' (Schein, 1991:252) and further emphasizes the distinction between cultural surface and depth in the vertical three-level model. The symbolic perspective talks about webs of meaning, organized in terms of symbols and representations (Smircich, 1985:63), also stating that webs of meaning are behind the immediate expressions of culture. The conceptualization of culture as depth implies that not all cultural levels and concepts are of equal importance, and within both perspectives the deeper and important cultural patterns are those that are most profound, invisible and taken for granted by the members of the organization.

These deep patterns of assumptions and meanings are expressed through a number of more superficial cultural manifestations. The superficial cultural manifestations may comprise physical objects, company statements, values, organizational events, stories, rituals, myths and the like. Within both perspectives, the discovery of the pattern of basic assumptions or webs of meaning makes it possible to decipher the contents of values and artifacts (functionalism) or to understand which cultural meanings are ascribed to the cultural expressions (symbolism). An artifact, an event, a gesture is never what it seems to be, but is analyzed or interpreted on the basis of an underlying pattern of assumptions or meanings held by members of the organization.

Hence, both perspectives conceive of culture as a set of stable relations between the visible and audible cultural manifestations and the underlying systems of assumptions or meanings, turning a multiplicity of cultural manifestations into representations of the same pattern of assumptions or meanings. Accordingly, the cultural manifestations are assumed never to be hollow: they do represent basic assumptions or symbolize the organizational members' essential patterns of meaning. Furthermore, a new set of assumptions and meanings will always emerge and replace old ones that are wearing thin from new organizational experiences.

The assumption of a relationship between the cultural depth and the more superficial manifestations of culture has first of all been criticized within the postmodern debate. Postmodernism obliterates the assumption of stable relationships between cultural manifestations (forms) and deep meanings, as postmodernism focuses on the rupture of the stable relations between culture's manifestations and underlying patterns of meaning (Jameson, 1983). From a postmodern point of view, cultural manifestations such as visible organizational structures, rituals, stories, metaphors, etc. appear isolated from the fragments of meaning created by the members of the organization (Jameson, 1983). Postmodernism holds no assumption of stable and meaningful patterns in organizations, manifestating themselves at the organizational surface. A cultural manifestation, like the ritual, is what it seems to be: a hard and repetitious superficial series of behavioral acts without any fixed underlying system of meaning. As such, postmodernism poses new questions in the analysis of cultural manifestations.

One question relates to the previous discussion about ambiguity, that is, whether the meaning of a ritual is changing and unpredictable and, thus, discontinuous. Is the same repeated behavior the manifestation of different and fluctuating meanings and interpretations? Members of the organization interpret the manifestation differently: some are confused, some have a clear notion of what's going on, others disagree. No fixed meaning exists (Martin and Meyerson, 1988; March and Olsen, 1976). Another question is whether the cultural manifestations have lost any meaning to the members of the organization and have been transformed into a threatening or alluring 'unreal' phenomenon. Here, the cultural manifestations become free-floating in the organization, like meaningless, weightless objects, leaving the organizational members with an intense feeling of strangeness (Jameson, 1983; Baudrillard, 1988). Hereby, postmodernism challenges the concept of culture in general, as it leaves nothing but accidental intersections between what has been labelled as cultural manifestations and whatever assumptions and meanings organizational members may hold at a given point in time.

Summary

The similarities between functionalism and symbolism are to a large extent shared by most cultural studies within both organizational theory and anthropology. The notion of culture as pattern(s) that are developed, learned and transmitted among members of organizations, has been taken for granted by most culture researchers and has focused their attention on the more regular and habitual aspects of organizational life. Also, the assumption of relations between the deep, underlying cultural patterns and the more superficial expressions of culture has dominated both perspectives, whether the relations have been elaborated within a predefined vertical model or have been explored in the study of associated symbolic expressions.

These similarities have been challenged by concepts of ambiguity and the critique from postmodernism, posing a number of new questions in the analysis of organizational culture. Almost by definition, the opportunities of constructing alternative frameworks in the study of organizational culture are very limited within postmodernism, as postmodernism has first of all intended to criticize and deconstruct existing knowledge (Martin, 1991, Smircich and Calas, 1987). In contrast, the challenge from the concept of ambiguity holds a range of opportunities for future studies of organizational culture, which are still in the making (Frost et al., 1991). So far, cultural ambiguity has been studied within the same conceptual frameworks as both the integration and fragmentation perspective (Martin and Meyerson, 1988) and concepts from symbolism (Hatch, 1993; Rosen, 1985), but future research may come up with totally new conceptual frameworks in order to fully analyze the unique features of ambiguity. Also, it has been argued (Kreiner and Schultz, 1993) that the 'ambiguous' character of organizational culture may be found in the interplay been the simultaneous existence of shared symbols and a multiplicity of local interpretations of these symbols. Thus, rather than restricting the cultural variety in organization, the existence of shared symbols works as tools for licensing cultural multiplicity. Thus, future studies may well develop the understanding of the ambiguous character of symbols themselves and the implications to organizational analysis.

Appendix 1
Organizational Diagrammes

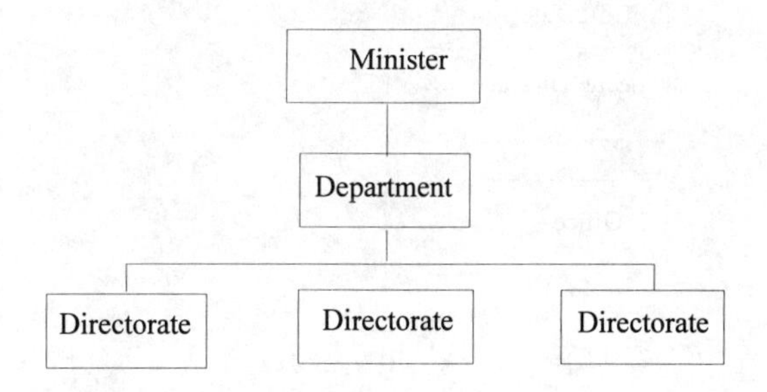

Diagramme 1. The Ministry

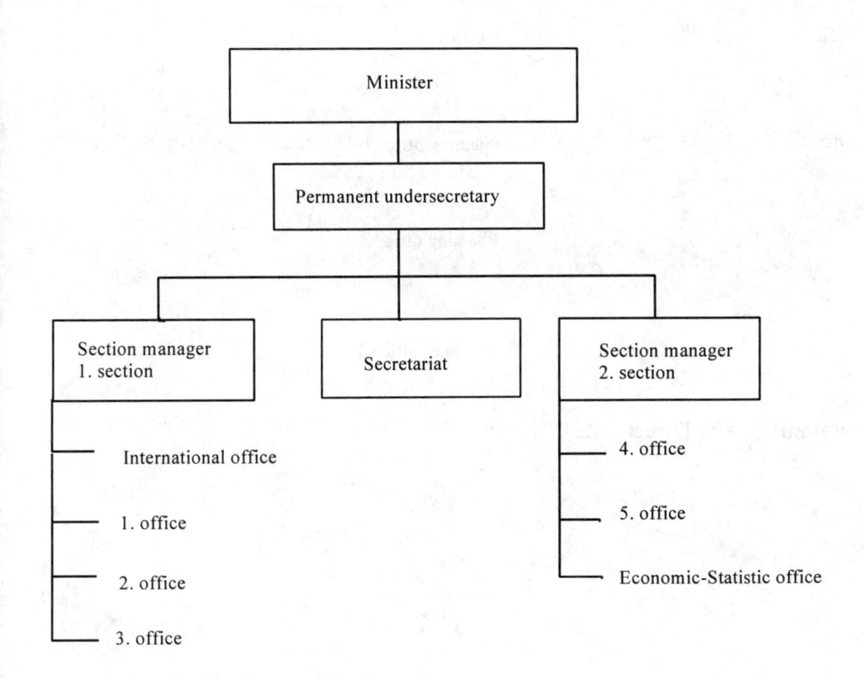

Diagramme 2. The Department

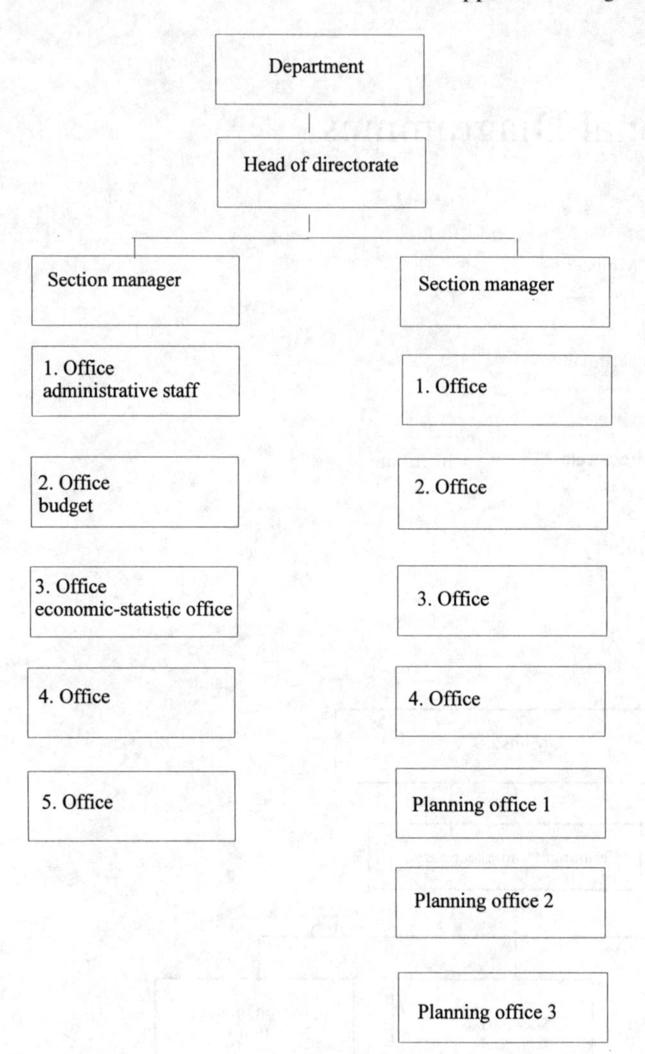

Diagramme 3. The Directorate

Appendix 2
Interviews and Observation Data

Interview data comprises interviews with employees in the department and the directorate, and interviews with external informants related to the directorate. Finally, observation data comprises meetings in the ministry.

Interviews

The data material was collected during two series of interviews: The first and most comprehensive series of interviews comprises staff members in the department and the directorate. The second and more limited series of interviews were conducted after a midway seminar and only comprises a few personal interviews and group interviews with the two organizations' AC-club (academic staff). All interviewees in the department and the directorate were guaranteed that they would not be quoted in the report. However, most interviews were recorded. The series of interviews comprise:

The first series of interviews:

Department:	16 interviews with managers and staff members, i.e. the manager and an academic staff member from each section unit.
Directorate:	22 interviews with managers and staff members, i.e. the manager and an academic staff member from section 1; the manager and an academic staff member from section 2 (except for two section units).

Individual interviews were conducted on the basis of the basic interview guide. The interviews were unstructured and adapted to the situation of the particular individual. On average the interviews lasted two hours. A few of the interviews with top managers stretched over two times two hours.

The second series of interviews:

Department: 4 interviews with managers. Group interview with the AC-club.

Directorate: 3 interviews with managers. Group interview with the AC-club.

The interviews lasted approximately one hour.

Interview with External Informants

15 interviews with key persons from:
– municipal organizations;
– organizations within the sector;
– other ministries;
– institutions of research and education.

Each interview was based on a specific interview guide due to the very different relationship of the informants to the ministry. The interviews typically lasted two hours and were not recorded.

Observations

Department: 2 months' observation of weekly meetings:
– X-meeting between the minister and the executive group.
– Y-meeting between head of department, chief of a section, head of administration and head of office.

Directorate: Participant observation at the group of managers' annual two-day seminar.

References

Abravanal, H. (1983): Mediatory Myths in the Service of Organizational Ideology; Pondy, L., Frost P., Morgan, G. & Dandridge, T. (eds): *Organizational Symbolism*, Greenwich, London, JAI Press.

Allaire, Y. & Firsirotu, M. (1984): Theories of Organizational Culture; *Organization Studies,* 5 (3).

Allen, R.F. (1985): Four Phases for Bringing about Cultural change; Kilmann, R., Saxton, M., Serpa, R. and Associates (eds): *Gaining Control of the Corporate Culture*, San Francisco, London, Jossey-Bass Publishers.

Alvesson, M. & Berg, P.O. (1992): *Corporate Culture and Organizational Symbolism*, Berlin, New York, Walter de Gruyter.

Argyris, C. (1982): The Executive Mind and Double-Loop Learning; *Organizational Dynamics*, Autumn.

Argyris, C. & Schoen, D. (1978): *Organizational Learning: A Theory of Action Perspective*, Reading, Mass., Addison Wesley.

Barley, S. (1983): Semiotics and the Study of Occupational and Organizational Cultures; *Administrative Science Quarterly*, 28 (3).

Barthes, R. (1990): *Mythologies*, New York, Noonday Press.

Baudrillard, J. (1988): *Selected Writings*, Stanford, Stanford University Press.

Bennis, W.G., Benne, K.D. & Chin, R. (eds) (1973): *The Planning of Change*, London, Holt, Rinehart & Winston.

Berg, P.O. (1986): Symbolic Management of Human Resources; *Human Resource Management*, 25 (4).

Berg, P.O. (1985): Organization Change as a Symbolic Transformation Process; Frost, P., Moore, L., Louis, M.R., Lundberg, C. & Martin, J. (eds): *Organizational Culture*, Beverly Hills, London, New Delhi, Sage Publications.

Berg, P.O. & Kreiner, K. (1992): Corporate Architecture: Turning Physical Settings into Symbolic Resources; Gagliardi. P. (ed): *Symbols and Artifacts. Views of the Corporate Landscape*, New York, Aldine de Gruyter.

Berg, P.O. & Porras, J. (1978): The Impact of Organizational Development; *Academy of Management Review*, 3 (2).

Berger, P.L. & Luckmann, T. (1966): *The Social Construction of Reality: A Treatise on the Sociology of Knowledge*, Garden City, New York, Doubleday.

Berthelsen, J. (ed) (1974): *Fortælleteori*, Copenhagen, Arena.

Blumer, H. (1962): Society as Symbolic Interaction; Rose, A. (ed): *Human Behavior and Social Processes*, Boston, Houghton Mifflin.

Bolman, L.G. & Deal, T.E. (1987): *Modern Approaches to Understanding and Managing Organizations*, San Francisco, London, Jossey-Bass Publishers.

Bormann, E.G. (1983): Symbolic Convergence: Organizational Communication and Culture; Putnam, L. & Pacanowsky, M.E. (eds): *Communication and Organizations*, Beverly Hills, London, New Delhi, Sage Publications.

Brandt-Pedersen, F. & Rønn-Poulsen, A. (1980): *Metodebogen*, Kolding, Nøgleforlaget.

Broms, H. & Gahmberg, H.H (1987): *Semiotics of Management*, Helsinki, Helsinki School of Economics, C: 53.

Broms, H. & Gahmberg, H.H (1983): Communication to Self in Organizations and Cultures; *Administrative Science Quarterly*, 28 (3).

Brown, D.L. (1983): *Managing Conflict at Organizational Interfaces*, Reading, Mass., Addison Wesley.

Brown, R.H. (1977): *A Poetic for Sociology*, Chicago and London, The University of Chicago Press.

Burrell, G. (1988): Modernism, Postmodernism and Organizational Analysis 2: The Contribution of Michel Foucault; *Organization Studies,* 9 (2).

Burrell, G. & Morgan, G. (1979): *Sociological Paradigms and Organizational Analysis*, London, Heinemann.

Cassirer, E. (1944): *An Essay of Man*, New Haven, Yale University Press.

Christensen, J.G. (1984): *Centraladministrationen: Organisation og politisk placering*, Copenhagen, Jurist-og Økonomforbundets forlag.

Christensen, S. & Kreiner, K. (1984): On the Origin of Organizational Cultures; Paper prepared for the First International Conference on Organizational Symbolism and Corporate Culture, Lund.

Christensen, S. & Molin, J. (1983): *Organisationskulturer*, Copenhagen, Akademisk Forlag.

Christensen, S., Jacobsen, P., Holt Larsen, H. & Molin, J. (1984): *Carlzons Klister*, Copenhagen, Forlaget Valmuen.

Clark, B.R. (1977) The Organizational Saga in Higher Education; *Administrative Science Quarterly*, 17 (2).

Cohen, A. (1985): *The Symbolic Construction of Community*, London, Tavistock Publications.

Cohen, A. (1976): *Two-dimensional Man*, Berkeley, Los Angeles, University of California Press.

Collin, F. (1987): *Organisationskultur og forandring*, Copenhagen, Nyt fra Samfundsvidenskaberne

Cooper, B. & Burell, G. (1988): Modernism, Postmodernism and Organizational Analysis: An Introduction; *Organization Studies,* 9 (1).

Crozier, M. (1964): *The Bureaucratic Phenomenon*, Chicago, University of Chicago Press.

Czarniawska-Joerges, B. (1992): *Styrningens Paradoxer*, Stockholm, Nordstedts.

Czarniawska-Joerges, B. (1988): *At Handla med Ord*, Stockholm, Carlssons.

Daft, R. (1983): Symbols in Organizations: A Dual-contents Framework of Analysis; Pondy, L., Frost P., Morgan, G. & Dandridge, T. (eds): *Organizational Symbolism*, Greenwich, London, JAI Press.

Dandridge, T. (1983): Symbols Function and Use; Pondy, L., Frost P., Morgan, G. & Dandridge, T. (eds): *Organizational Symbolism,* Greenwich, London, JAI Press.

Deal, T.E. & Kennedy, A. (1982): *Corporate Cultures*, Reading, Mass., Addison Wesley.

Denyson, D. (1990): *Corporate Culture and Organizational Effectiveness*, New York, John Wiley and Sons.

Durkheim, E. (1972): *Den sociologiske metode*, Copenhagen, Fremad.

Dyer, W.G. (1985): The Cycle of Cultural Evolution in Organizations; Kilmann, R., Saxton, M., Serpa, R. and Associates (eds): *Gaining Control of the Corporate Culture*, San Francisco, London, Jossey-Bass Publishers.

Dyer, W.G. (1984): Culture in Organizations: A Case Study and Analysis; Working paper, Boston, Sloan School of Management, MIT.

Evered, R. (1983): The Language of Organizations: The Case of the Navy; Pondy, L., Frost P., Morgan, G. & Dandridge, T. (eds): *Organizational Symbolism*, Greenwich, London, JAI Press.

Feldman, M. (1989): *Order without Design. Information Processing and Policy Making*, Palo Alto, CA., Stanford University Press.

Festinger, L.A. (1957): *A Theory of Cognitive Dissonance*, Stanford, Stanford University Press.

Filby, I. & Willmott, H. (1988): Ideologies and Contradictions in a Public Relations Department: The Seduction and Impotence of Living Myth; *Organization Studies*, 9 (3).

Finansministeriet (1986): *Modernisering af ministeriernes økonomistyring*, Copenhagen, Budgetdepartementet.

Finansministeriet (1983): *Redegørelse til folketinget om regeringens program for modernisering af den offentlige sektor*, Copenhagen, Budgetdepartementet.

French W.L. & Bell, C.H. (1990): *Organizational Development*, 4th edition, Englewood Cliffs, Prentice-Hall.

French, W.L. & Zawacki (ed) (1983): *Organizational Development. Theory, Practice, Research*, Texas, Business Publications.

Frost, P. & Krefting, L. (1985): Untangling Webs, Surfing Wawes, and Wildcatting: A Multi-Metaphor Perspective on Managing Organizational Culture; Frost, P., Moore, L., Louis, M.R., Lundberg, C. & Martin, J. (eds): *Organizational Culture*, Beverly Hills, London, New Delhi, Sage Publications.

Frost, P. & Morgan, G. (1983): Symbols and Sensemaking: The Realization of a Framework; Pondy, L., Frost P., Morgan, G. & Dandridge, T. (eds): *Organizational Symbolism*, Greenwich, London, JAI Press.

Frost, P., Moore, L., Louis, M.R., Lundberg, C. & Martin, J. (1991): *Reframing Organizational Culture*, Newbury Park, London, New Delhi, Sage Publications.

Frost, P., Moore, L., Louis, M.R., Lundberg, C. & Martin, J. (1985): *Organizational Culture*, Beverly Hills, London, New Delhi, Sage Publications.

Gagliardi, P. (ed) (1992): *Symbols and Artifacts. Views of the Corporate Landscape*, New York, Aldine de Gruyter.

Gahmberg, H. (1986): *Symbols and Values of Strategic Managers – A Semiotic Approach*, Helsinki, Acta Academia, A: 47.

Geertz, C. (1988): *Works and Lives. The Anthropologist as Author*, Stanford, CA, Stanford University Press.

Geertz, C. (1983): *Local Knowledge*, New York, Basic Books.

Geertz, C. (1973): *Interpretation of Cultures*, New York, Basic Books.

Gioia, D. & Pitre, E. (1990): Multiparadigm Perspectives on Theory Building; *Academy of Management Review*, 15 (4).

Glaser, B. & Strauss, A. (1967): *The Discovery of Grounded Theory*, Chicago, Aldine Publishing Company.

Goffman, E. (1959): *The Presentation of Self in Everyday Life*, New York, Doubleday.

Gregory, K. (1983): Native-View Paradigms: Multiple Cultures and Culture Conflicts in Organizations; *Administrative Science Quarterly*, 28 (3).

Hampden-Turner, C. (1990): *Creating Corporate Culture. From Discord to Harmony*, Reading, Mass., Addison-Wesley.

Hatch, M.J. (1993): The Dynamics of Organizational Culture: Integrating Schein's Model with Symbolic-interpretive Perspectives; *Academy of Management Review*, 18 (4).

Hatch, M.J. & Ehrlich, S.B. (1993): Spontaneous Humor as an Indicator of Paradox and Ambiguity in Organizations; *Organization Studies*, 14 (4).

Hirsch, P.M. & Andrews, J.A. (1983): Ambushes, Shootouts and Knights of the Roundtable: The Language of Corporate Takeovers; Pondy, L., Frost P., Morgan, G. & Dandridge, T. (eds): *Organizational Symbolism*, Greenwich, London, JAI Press.

Hofstede, G. (1991): *Cultures and Organizations. Software of the Mind*, London, McGraw-Hill Book Company.

Hofstede, G. (1980): *Culture's Consequences*, Beverly Hills, London, New Delhi, Sage Publications.

Hofstede, G., Neuijen, B., Ohavy, D.D. & Sanders, G. (1990): Measuring Organizational Culture: A Qualitative and Quantitative Study across Twenty Cases; *Administrative Science Quarterly*, 35 (2).

Huff, A. S. (1983): A Rhetorical Examination of Strategic Change; Pondy, L., Frost P., Morgan, G. & Dandridge, T. (eds): *Organizational Symbolism*, Greenwich, London, JAI Press.

Jameson, F. (1983): Postmodernism and Consumer Society; Foster H. (ed): *Postmodern Culture*, London, Pluto Press.

Jørgensen, T.B. (1981): *Samspil og konflikt mellem organisationer*, Copenhagen, Nyt fra Samfundsvidenskaberne.

Kilmann, R., Saxton, M., Serpa, R. and Associates (eds)(1985): *Gaining Control of the Corporate Culture*, San Francisco, London, Jossey-Bass Publishers.

Kluckholm, C. & Strodtbeck, F.L. (1961): *Variations in Value Orientation*, New York, Harper & Row.

Kotter, J. & Heskett, J. (1992): *Corporate Culture and Performance*, New York, The Free Press.

Kreiner, K. & Schultz, M. (1993): Soft Cultures. The Symbolism of Cross-border Organizing; Paper presented at the Academy of Management, Atlanta, August.

Kroeber, A.L. & Kluckholm, C. (1963): *Culture: A Critical Review of Concepts and Definitions*, New York, Vintage.

Kuhn, T. (1962): *The Structure of Scientific Revolutions*, Chicago, University of Chicago Press.

Kunda, G. (1991): *Engineering Culture: Control and Commitment in a High-tech Corporation*, Philadelphia, Temple University Press.

Larsen, J. & Schultz, M. (1992): Artifacts within a Bureaucratic Monastery; Gagliardi, P. (ed): *Symbols and Artifacts: Views of the Corporate Landscape*, New York, Aldine de Gruyter.

Leavitt, H. J. (1965): Applied Organizational Change in Industry: Structural, Technological and Humanistic Approaches; James G. March: *Handbook of Organizations*, Chicago, Rand McNally.

Levi-Strauss, C. (1968): *Structural Anthropology*, London, The Penguin Press.

Lewin, K. (1951): *Field Theory in Social Science*, New York, Harper & Row.

Lindblom, C. & Cohen, M. (1979): *Usable Knowledge. Social Science and Social Problem Solving*, New Haven, Yale University Press.

Lindstead, S. (1986): Fictions. A Methodological Discussion Paper; Paper presented at Workshop in Conference on Organizational Symbolism and Corporate Culture, Hull, University of Hull, August.

Louis, M.R. (1983): Organizations as Cultural Bearing Milieux; Pondy, L., Frost P., Morgan, G. & Dandridge, T. (eds): *Organizational Symbolism*, Greenwich, London, JAI Press.

Lundberg, C.G. (1985): On the Feasibility of Cultural Intervention in Organizations; Frost, P., Moore, L., Louis, M.R., Lundberg, C. & Martin, J. (eds): *Organizational Culture*, Beverly Hills, London, New Delhi, Sage Publications.

March, J.G. & Olsen, J.P. (eds) (1976): *Ambiguity and Choice in Organizations*, Bergen, Universitetsforlaget.

Martin, J. (1993): *Cultures in Organizations. Three Perspectives*, New York, Oxford, Oxford University Press.

Martin, J. (1990): Deconstructing Organizational Taboos: The Suppression of Gender Conflict in Organizations; *Organization Science*, 1 (1).

Martin, J. (1985): Can Organizational Culture be Managed?; Frost, P., Moore, L., Louis, M.R., Lundberg, C. & Martin, J. (eds): *Organizational Culture*, Beverly Hills, London, New Delhi, Sage Publications.

Martin, J. & Meyerson, D. (1988): Organizational Cultures and the Denial, Channelling and Acknowledgement of Ambiguity; Pondy, L., Boland, R. & Thomas, H. (eds): *Managing Ambiguity and Change*, New York, John Wiley and Sons.

Martin, J. & Siehl, C. (1983): Organizational Culture and Counter Culture: An Uneasy Symbiosis; *Organizational Dynamics*, Autumn.

Martin, J., Feldman, M., Hatch, M.J. & Sitkin, S.B. (1983): The Uniqueness Paradox in Organizational Stories; *Administrative Science Quarterly*, 28 (3).

Meyer, J. & Rowan, B. (1977): Institutionalized Organizations: Formal Structure as Myth and Ceremony; *American Journal of Sociology*, 83 (2).

Meyer, J.W. & Scott, W.R. (ed) (1983): *Organizational Environments*, Beverly Hills, London, New Delhi, Sage Publications.

Meyerson, D. (1991): "Normal" Ambiguity? A Glimpse of an Occupational Culture; Frost, P., Moore, L., Louis, M.R., Lundberg, C. & Martin, J. (eds): *Reframing Organizational Culture,* Newbury Park, London, New Delhi, Sage Publications.

Meyerson, D. (1989): The Social Construction of Ambiguity and Burnout: A Study of Hospital Social Workers; Ph.D. Dissertation, Stanford, Stanford University.

Meyerson, D. & Martin, J. (1987): Cultural Change: An Integration of Three Different Views; *Journal of Management Studies*, 24 (6).

Mills, C.W. (1959, 1980): *The Sociological Imagination*, London, Penguin Books.

Mintzberg, H. (1979): *The Structuring of Organizations*, Englewood Cliffs, Prentice-Hall.

Molin, J. (1987): *Beyond Structure and Rationality*, Copenhagen, Akademisk Forlag.

Molin, J. & Molin, S. (1988): *Den iscenesatte virkelighed,* Copenhagen, Akademisk Forlag.

Morgan, G. (1986): *Images of Organization*, Beverly Hills, London, New Delhi, Sage Publications.

Olins, W. (1989): *Corporate Identity*, London, Thames & Hudson.

Ortner, S.B. (1973): On Key Symbols; *American Anthropologist*, 75 (5).

Ouchi, W.G. (1981): *Theory Z*, Reading, Mass., Addison Wesley.

Parsons, T. (1951): *The Social System*, Glencoe, The Free Press.

Pascale, R.T & Athos, A.G. (1982): *The Art of Japanese Management: Applications for American Executives*, New York, Warner.

Pedersen, J.S. & Sørensen, J. (1989): *Organisational Cultures in Theory and Practice*, Aldershot, Avery.

Perniola, M. (1982): *Blændværker*, Aarhus, Sjakalen.

Peters, T. & Waterman, R.H. (1982): *In Search of Excellence*, New York, Harper & Row.

Pondy, L. (1983): The Role of Metaphors and Myths in Organization and in the Facilitation of Change; Pondy, L., Frost, P., Morgan, G. & Dandridge, T. (eds): *Organizational Symbolism*, Greenwich, London, JAI Press.

Pondy, L., Frost, P., Morgan, G. & Dandridge, T. (eds) (1983): *Organizational Symbolism*, Greenwich, London, JAI Press.

Putnam, L. (1983): The Interpretative Perspective: An Alternative to Functionalism; Putnam, L. & Pacanowsky, M.E. (eds): *Communication and Organizations*, Beverly Hills, London, New Delhi, Sage Publications.

Putnam, L. & Pacanowsky, M.E. (1983): Introduction; Putnam, L. & Pacanowsky, M.E. (eds): *Communication and Organizations*, Beverly Hills, London, New Delhi, Sage Publications.

Radcliff-Brown, A.R. (1952): *Structure and Function in Primitive Society*, Glencoe, The Free Press.

Raelin, J. (1991): *The Clash of Cultures*, Boston, Harvard Business School Press.

Raspa, D. (1992): The C.E.O. as Corporate Myth-Makes: Negotiating the Boundaries of Work and Play at Domino's Pizza Company; Gagliardi, P. (ed): *Symbols and Artifacts. Views of the Corporate Landscape*, New York, Aldine de Gruyter.

Ritzer, G. (1975): *Sociology – A Multiple Paradigm Science*, Boston, Allyn & Bacon.

Rosen, M. (1985): Breakfast at Spiro's: Dramaturgy and Dominance; *Journal of Management,* 11 (2).

Sapienza, A. (1985): Believing is Seeing: How Culture Influences the Decisions Top Managers Take; Kilmann, R., Saxton, M., Serpa, R. and Associates (eds): *Gaining Control of the Corporate Culture*, San Francisco, London, Jossey-Bass Publishers.

Sayle, M. (1983): The Yellow Peril and the Red Haired Devils; *Harpers*, November.

Schein, E. (1992): *Organizational Culture and Leadership*, 2nd edition, San Francisco, Jossey-Bass Publishers.

Schein, E. (1991): What is Culture?; Frost, P., Moore, L., Louis, M.R., Lundberg, C. & Martin, J. (eds): *Reframing Organizational Culture*, Newbury Park, London, New Delhi, Sage Publications.

Schein, E. (1987): *The Clinical Perspective in Fieldwork*, Newbury Park, Beverly Hills, London, New Delhi, A Sage University Paper, Sage Publications.

Schein, E. (1985a): *Organizational Culture and Leadership*; San Francisco, Washington, London, Jossey-Bass Publishers.

Schein, E. (1985b): How Culture Forms, Develops and Changes; Kilmann, R., Saxton, M., Serpa, R. and Associates (eds): *Gaining Control of the Corporate Culture*, San Francisco, London, Jossey-Bass Publishers.

Schein, E. (1984): Coming to a New Awareness of Organizational Culture; *Sloan Management Review*, 25 (2).

Schultz, M. (1992): Postmodern Pictures of Organizational Culture; *International Studies of Management and Organization,* 22 (2).

Schultz, M. (1991): Transitions Between Symbolic Domains in Organizations; *Organization Studies*, 12 (4).

Scott, W.R. (1992): *Organizations. Rational, Natural and Open Systems*, 3rd edition, Englewood Cliffs, Prentice-Hall.

Scott, W.R. (1990): Symbols and Organizations. From Barnard to the Institutionalists; Williamson, O. (ed): *Organization Theory: From Chester Barnard to the Present and Beyond*, New York, Oxford, Oxford University Press.

Silverman, D. (1971): *The Theory of Organizations. A Sociological Framework*, New York, Basic Books.

Smircich, L. (1985): Is the Concept of Culture a Paradigm for Understanding Organizations and Ourselves?; Frost, P., Moore, L., Louis, M.R., Lundberg, C. & Martin, J. (eds): *Organizational Culture*, Beverly Hills, London, New Delhi, Sage Publications.

Smircich, L. (1983a): Concepts of Organizational Culture and Organizational Analysis; *Administrative Science Quarterly*, 28 (3).

Smircich, L. (1983b): Organizations as Shared Meanings; Pondy, L., Frost, P., Morgan, G. & Dandridge, T. (eds): *Organizational Symbolism*, Greenwich, London, JAI Press.

Smircich, L. & Calas, M. (1987): Post-culture: Is the Organizational Culture Literature Dominant but Dead?; Paper for the Third International Conference on Organizational Symbolism and Corporate Culture, Milan, June.

Smircich, L. & Morgan, G. (1982): Leadership: The Management of Meaning; *The Journal of Applied Behavioral Science*, 18 (3).

Sørensen, W. (1983): *Uden mål – og med*, Copenhagen, Gyldendal.

Spradley, J. (1979): *The Ethnographic Interview*, Florida, Holt, Rinehart & Winston.

Thyssen, O. (1987): *Påfuglens øjne – efter postmodernismen*, Copenhagen, Rosinante.

Toffler, A. (1980): *The Third Wave*, New York, William Morrow.

Trice, H.M. & Beyer, J.M. (1993): *The Cultures of Work Organizations*, Englewood Cliffs, Prentice Hall.

Trice, H.M. & Beyer, J.M. (1985): Using Six Organizational Rites to Change Culture; Kilmann, R., Saxton, M., Serpa, R. and Associates (eds): *Gaining Control of the Corporate Culture*, San Francisco, London, Jossey-Bass Publishers.

Trice, H.M. & Beyer, J.M. (1984): Studying Organizational Cultures through Rites and Ceremonials; *Academy of Management Review*, 9 (4).

Tunstall, W.B. (1985): Breakup the Bell System: A Case Study in Cultural Transformation; Kilmann, R., Saxton, M., Serpa, R. and Associates (eds): *Gaining Control of the Corporate culture*, San Francisco, London, Jossey-Bass Publishers.

Turner, B.A. (ed) (1990): *Organizational Symbolism*, Berlin, New York, Walter de Gruyter.

Turner, B.A. (1981): Some Practical Aspects of Qualitative Data Analysis: One Way of Organizing the Cognitive Processes Associated with the Generation of Grounded Theory; *Quality and Quantity,* 15 (3).

Turner, V. & Turner, E. (1978): Notes on Processual Symbolic Analysis; Turner, V. & Turner, E. (eds): *Image and Pilgrimage in Christian Culture*, New York, Columbia University Press.

Turner, V.W. (1967a): *The Forest of Symbols: Aspects of Ndembu Ritual*, Ithaca, N.Y., Cornell University Press.

Turner, V.W. (1967b): Betwixt and Between: The Liminal Period in Rites of Passage; Turner, V.W.: *The Forest of Symbols: Aspects of Ndembu Ritual*, Ithaca, N.Y., Cornell University Press.

Van Maanen, J. (1988): *Tales of the Field: On Writing Ethnography*, Chicago, University of Chicago Press.

Van Maanen, J. & Barley, S. (1985): Cultural Organization: Fragments of a Theory; Frost, P., Moore, L., Louis, M.R., Lundberg, C. & Martin, J. (eds): *Organizational Culture*, Beverly Hills, London, New Delhi, Sage Publications.

Vogel, E. (1979): *Japan as Number One*, Cambridge, Mass, Harvard University Press.

Weick, K. (1969): *The Social Psychology of Organizing*; Reading, Mass., Addison Wesley.

Westerlund, G. & Sjøstrand, S. (1979): *Organizational Myths*, New York, Harper & Row.

Wilkins, A. (1983): Organizational Stories as Symbols which Control the Organization; Pondy, L., Frost, P., Morgan, G. & Dandridge, T. (eds): *Organizational Symbolism*, Greenwich, London, JAI Press.

Williamson, J. (1978): *Decoding Advertisements. Ideology and Meaning in Advertising*, London, Marion Boyars.

Witkin, R.W. & Poupart, R. (1985): Running Commentary on Imaginatively Re--lived Events. A Method for Obtaining Qualitative Rich Data; *Trento Quaderno*, 15 (6).

Index